M000318237

Letters to Matt

A mother's tender journey to
find herself after battling her son's
7-year addiction, overdose and death

MARY BETH CICHOCKI, R.N.

Letters to Matt – 1st ed.
MaryBeth Cichocki, R.N.
mothersheartbreak.com

Cover Design by AlyBlue Media, LLC
Interior Design by AlyBlue Media LLC
Published by AlyBlue Media, LLC

Copyright © 2020 by AlyBlue Media All rights reserved. No part of this publication
may be reproduced, distributed, or transmitted in any form
or by any means, without prior written permission of the publisher.

ISBN: 978-1-950712-29-8
AlyBlue Media, LLC
Ferndale, WA 98248
www.AlyBlueMedia.com

This book is designed to provide informative narrations to readers. It is sold with the
understanding that the author and publisher are not engaged to render any type of
psychological, legal, or any other kind of professional advice. The content is the sole
expression and opinion of the author. No warranties or guarantees are expressed or
implied by the choice to include any of the content in this book. Neither the publisher
nor the author shall be liable for any physical, psychological, emotional, financial, or
commercial damages including but not limited to special, incidental, consequential, or
other damages.

PRINTED IN THE UNITED STATES OF AMERICA

Testimonials

MaryBeth's journey through the loss of her son highlights the devastating impact that addiction has on the lives of so many people, not just the person battling the disease. As chronicled in this book, channeling her grief into relentless advocacy, she has been instrumental in the creation and passage of new laws addressing substance use disorder. —STEPHANIE L. HANSEN, Delaware State Senator, 10th District

By turning her pain into purpose, MaryBeth's journey recounts the heartbreak of countless American families who've experienced the tragedy of the overdose crisis. Her love for Matt transcends off the page and into the soul of every single loved one who shares this common heartbreak. —RYAN HAMPTON, Activist and author of *American Fix: Inside the Opioid Addiction Crisis—and How to End It*

MaryBeth's journey through her son's addiction to the ultimate loss of his life is a heartbreaking one, to say the least. MaryBeth is a warrior mother who has, and still does, offer her grief to support one more family lost in the same crisis. This book is a must read! —TIM RYAN, Thought Leader, Dope To Hope LLC

Letters to Matt is a powerful book that voices what many of us feel after loss of our child yet too afraid to say aloud. A definite must read for anyone who has lost a child. —LYNDA CHELDELIN FELL, International Grief Institute

Letters to Matt

Contents

Letters to Matt

Foreword

Five-plus years. It's been five-plus years since MaryBeth Cichocki lost her son, Matt, to a prescription pain medication overdose.

Matt was prescribed medication following back surgery that left him in constant pain. Instead of finding ways to help him manage that pain, doctors kept prescribing pain medication. In time, Matt found his own sources.

MaryBeth did everything she could to help her son battle his opioid addiction. Everything. For seven years.

She was there from the very beginning encouraging him to stop, cut back, do other things to relieve the pain. She was there when he went to rehab, and there when he came out, determined to get his life back on track. She was there with all her love to do it all again when Matt relapsed five times. She never gave up and was thrilled when he decided to go to a sober living home after his last rehab—the horrors of which you'll learn reading this book.

But like her son and much of society, MaryBeth didn't understand just how complicated addiction is as a chronic, often relapsing brain disease. Like other chronic diseases, such as heart disease and diabetes, its treatment requires a comprehensive medical approach to manage.

MaryBeth followed what other parents have done to help their kids—she kept trying. Through it all, she believed with all her might that her son would recover and their lives would return to normal.

That hope was shattered January 3, 2015, at 12:15 p.m. when her husband showed up at the hospital where MaryBeth worked as a nurse caring for ill babies.

"It's Matt. He's dead," her husband said through streaming tears.

MaryBeth describes what happened next. "I remember a feeling of leaving my body to escape the pain as my heart was breaking. I remember someone screaming, never thinking it was me...."

And then her hell began.

Letters to Matt chronicles MaryBeth's journey through grief in letters she wrote to her son following his death. Raw, uncensored, and heartbreaking, MaryBeth explains to Matt how she's trying to find her footing in life. She lost her job, close friends, and family because she couldn't grieve in a manner others could be comfortable with.

She also lost her sense of self and gives words to her pain, writing sentences like, "Our culture sees grief as a mess that needs to be cleaned up. I see grief as something that now lives inside my soul."

Yet MaryBeth's letters also give us hope. As the years passed, she found a way to channel her grief, anger, and pain into helping others. As she writes to Matt, "I still grieve you every day but now feel like as long as I have my advocacy, your death will always have meaning."

Her advocacy work has culminated in the passage of six legislative bills that have changed how Delaware treats those who suffer from addiction. She writes a blog, and her articles appear in countless magazines. She started A Hug From Matt, a nonprofit delivering backpacks and hugs to homeless youth, and formed a support group for parents who have lost a child to the misunderstood disease of addiction. She calls it SAAD, Support After Addiction Death.

I've known MaryBeth since Matt died, and am continually awed by her courage, strength, hope, and marvel at her gift for penning the ugly side of addiction—the side thousands of parents have experienced but don't know how to talk about or live through.

Letters to Matt is for all parents whose lives have been shattered by the death of their child to addiction.

LISA FREDERIKSEN
Speaker, consultant, founder of BreakingTheCycles.com, and author of the 10th Anniversary Edition *If You Loved Me, You'd Stop! What you really need to know when your loved one drinks too much*

Preface

My letters to Matt began on a cold day in February. The weather mimicked my mood—dark and gloomy. It was one of those days when my heart ached badly from the loss of Matt and the future I'd imagined for us both. I just needed him to be here. I needed a do-over. I needed to talk to him and let him know how his death shattered my life.

I was sitting alone at my laptop and started to compose a letter to Matt. As I typed and poured out my heart, I could feel his presence. I closed my eyes and could see his handsome face and incredible eyes.

I felt a connection I thought I had lost. I found such comfort as I wrote to Matt, letting him know what was happening in my life since his death.

The letters became my way of staying connected to Matt. I began to write weekly, keeping him updated on life here on earth. Writing these letters became my therapy. It gave me a way to include Matt in my daily life. Many days I would sit alone and feel like Matt and I were having the type of conversations we often had when he was alive.

Writing these letters reminded me of those catchup phone calls when we shared the daily happenings of our lives. These letters became a lifeline that kept me connected to my son beyond his death.

I never intended to publish my letters. I planned to keep them to myself but one day, another mother who lost her child asked to read what I had written to Matt. With tears in her eyes, she told me my letters touched her heart and gave her hope that she would survive her own loss, and I should share my letters with other grieving parents.

My hope is that these letters will give people permission to grieve without either guilt or a timeline to get over the death of their child. I want parents to understand that losing a child doesn't mean the connection is lost. I want parents to understand that our child will always live in our hearts, and though we will always grieve, our connection to our child will never die. ♥

I feel this book is essential for grieving parents. Society wants you to believe that if you survive all the firsts, your grief will disappear and life will return to normal. Society is uncomfortable with those who are struggling with grief.

I foolishly believed this theory until I lived through all those firsts, and found my grief was heavier than it was in the very beginning. I personally found that the second, third and fourth years were much harder than that first year. I realize now that I was in shock that first year. My brain was surrounded by a cocoon of fog that protected my mind from the ugly reality that Matt was really dead.

Many parents who lose a child suffer from what is called complicated grief. We not only grieve our children, we also grieve the future we will never have. We will never hear their voice again. They will never be coming home to introduce a new girlfriend or boyfriend. There will be no college graduations, weddings, or grandchildren. We are filled with guilt over things said and not said. Perhaps if had been kinder or more strict, our child would have survived.

Dr. Elisabeth Kübler-Ross wrote a book detailing the five stages of grief—denial, anger, bargaining, depression, and acceptance. In reality, grief follows no stages or pattern. It hits unexpectedly with a force that takes your breath away and drops you to your knees. Grief knows no timeline. It follows no pattern.

I want to give parents permission to grieve however they wish. I want them to understand that losing a child is unlike any other grief. I want parents to be kind to themselves and understand that life has been shattered and the passing of time makes no difference to the depths of their grief.

When people reminded me it had been a year and I should now be okay, I questioned myself and felt as though something was wrong with me. Then my anger would surface and I would think, *your child is alive, and you have no clue what my daily life is like.* I got tired of feeling guilty because I continued to grieve my son. My letters to Matt explain what it's like to be a grieving parent.

Writing these letters allowed me to express my continued grief without worrying about the judgement of those who have no clue as to how the loss of a child demolishes your life. It's okay to never be okay again. Parents must let grief come as it comes, and understand that the rollercoaster through all the different emotions is absolutely normal as they begin to navigate life without their precious child.

MARYBETH CICHOCKI
MothersHeartBreak.com

Matt's story

Have you ever met a guy who's smile would light up the room? Who made you feel like you found a long lost friend? The kind of guy who'd give you the shirt off his back, and bring every stray dog home and make it a member of the family?

That was my son, Matt. He had that happy-go-lucky personality that drew people in and made them fall in love. Unfortunately, Matt never loved himself enough.

Matt experimented with marijuana in high school. He loved the high. He ended up in his first rehab while in high school where he spent thirty days as an in-patient in Newport News, Virginia.

Foolishly, I thought we had beat his disease.

Matt went on to become an excellent mechanic. He moved to the beach, bought a home, and opened his business. His adult life appeared free of drugs. He was an adult. He was successful. I took a deep breath and started to relax. Matt loved life and was living it to the fullest.

The beginning of the end began with a back injury. Matt was lifting an engine when he felt a pop. The next day he could barely walk. He called to say he had seen his doctor who prescribed Percocet and told Matt to take it easy. I remember a cold chill running up my spine. Call it mother's intuition or a flashback to his younger days. Being a nurse, I knew the dangers of any form of opioids, and warned Matt to try to stay away.

I knew his pain was real. I also knew his predisposition to become addicted.

Months passed and the signs were all there, yet I was in denial. Missing days at his office. Unpaid bills. Not returning my phone calls. Our close relationship was changing as the disease found him again. I felt like I was living in Groundhog Day, except this time Matt was an adult. My hands were tied.

Matt struggled with his addiction for seven years. During that time, he lost everything he had worked so hard to gain. His business closed six months after his injury. He was abusing the pills and trying to continue to work on cars. It was obvious to his steady customers that something was terribly wrong, and they took business elsewhere.

Mortgage payments were missed and Matt's beach house was repossessed by the bank. Everything he loved was now gone.

He came home to me.

During those seven years, Matt was in and out of rehab. I referred to that time in our lives as the revolving doors of rehab. I felt like we were strapped on a rollercoaster holding on for the ride of our lives.

Matt's insurance never permitted him to stay in rehab the length of time needed to learn how to handle life without pills. He'd come home clean, and I would look into clear eyes and thank God that Matt was back. He was such a joy to be around. He never wanted to be that person who was tortured by cravings. Our life would just start to feel normal again, but the joy was short-lived. Within weeks, he returned to his world of numbness and the cycle would begin again.

Matt had a horrible fear of needles. This gave me the false sense of never having to worry about him graduating to heroin. Little did I realize that crushing and snorting Percocet was just as deadly.

Matt's last attempt to get and stay clean took place at a rehab close to home, Bowling Green in Kennett Square, Pennsylvania. I watched him struggle with the demons that plagued him most of his adult life. I was so proud and hopeful that Matt was coming back. His clear eyes and beautiful smile greeted me at each visit. I remember sitting together looking out over the water.

Matt was then going to Boca House, a recovery home in Florida. I was unsure about his decision yet every book I'd read about addiction spoke of different people, places and things being the best choice for new sobriety. Matt left for Florida on June 2, 2014. He wrapped me up in his big bearhug and told me he was so happy to have the monkey off his back. Little did I know that monkey would find him in Florida.

We spoke twice a day. I was going through withdrawals from seeing him, yet he was starting a new life. Once again he was living by the sea, his happy place. He found a job and his self-esteem returned. I allowed myself to believe that this was his ah-ha moment, that finally he was in a good place in his life.

Our last words were spoken on a Friday night. My ears trained to pick up cues found none.

"I love you. Mom."

"I love you, Matt."

For reasons my heart will never understand, Matt relapsed and lost the battle. On January 3, 2015, at 12:15 p.m., I heard the words that shattered my world.

"Matt is dead."

Since his death, I have been trying to pick up the pieces of my life. I started a support group for parents who, like me, have lost a piece of their heart. I began writing letters to Matt and started a blog called Mothers Heart Break. I share our story and educate others about the addictive properties of prescription opioids. I also started a Facebook page in his honor, Breaking the Stigma of Addiction: Matt's Story as a place to post educational articles about prescription drugs and their potential for abuse.

I would give anything for a do-over. To rewind time knowing what I know now. I would have held on tighter and never let him go.

YEAR 1

Letters to Matt

The Final Goodbye

Matt,

It's been four days since you died and my world has spun off its axis. I'm unbalanced now, walking around in a thick fog. Disbelief and reality take turns playing games with my heart.

Trying to bring you home has been a challenge. I was told it would be easier to cremate you in Florida. Quicker and cheaper. This mother needs to see you again. Part of me remains in denial. This is a horrific mix up. You are alive, and this son belongs to another mother.

They tell me your flight arrived in Philly late last night. The last time you were in Philly was to fly into a new life. You were so full of hope and dreams. I never expected you to return home in a box.

Flights have been off schedule because of back-to-back snow storms. Was that you, Matt? You always loved the snow.

I'm told I can see you today just for a bit as we now have a schedule to keep. I need to see your handsome face. A face that is now frozen in time. There will be no wrinkles or gray hair for you, my beautiful boy. We'll never dance together as you wed the love of your life. I'll never hold your child in my arms. My dreams about your future are torn to shreds, blowing away in the January wind.

I feel like an actress in a role I never wanted to play. What does a mother wear to go view the body of her son? My mind is foggy and my body feels like I'm walking through quicksand. Eyes swollen. Face puffy and red. I can't even look at my reflection. I don't care anymore.

I don't talk to Jesus. There is nothing to talk about. He didn't protect you, and neither did I. I've read that Jesus only gives you what you can handle. He doesn't know me like I thought he did. I always told him I could never survive losing you. And now you are gone.

I was able to spend two hours with you. It was the shortest two hours of my life. I needed to see you alone, before anyone else. I needed it to be just you and me, like it used to be.

A mother and her son hanging out and sharing life, except now your life is gone and I'm left behind.

Ray dropped me off and went to park his car. I walked inside and tried to catch my breath. I asked you to give me the strength I needed to see you today. To walk into a funeral home and say goodbye to my beautiful son.

The room was eerily quiet. I walked through my fog and felt the familiar feelings of my throat tightening up and heart racing envelope my body. I closed my eyes and prayed it wouldn't be your face my eyes would see. I would shout for joy, *it's not Matt, it's not Matt!* My fantasy was short-lived.

You looked like you were sleeping, quiet yet so cold. I could see the bluish color of your skin under the layer of makeup applied to your face. I grabbed your hand and ran my fingers through your hair. I laid my head on your chest, praying to hear the beat of your heart. *Oh, Go, this cannot be,* my brain silently screamed.

Slowly, Ray and Mike approached. I wouldn't move from holding you, my body frozen with yours. They ask why you were wet. I didn't realize my flood of tears was falling onto you face.

I wondered if you were looking down on your broken family. Your brother, once so strong, was now crying like a baby.

Our time was up. I wanted to stay forever. I wanted to sit with you until I am no more. Through my fog, I heard voices. "Mom, we need to go. Mom, please, let go."

I was surrounded by what was left of us. Mike and Ray gave me the strength to walk away. The slap of reality hit my face like a blast of icy wind on this most brutal of days.

I spend the next days planning your memorial. Denial is a wonderful thing. In all the years we battled your addiction, I never thought I would be planning your funeral. I felt betrayed.

In all the books I had read that were written by parents like me, the addict lived. Everyone had a happy ending. *Beautiful Boy, An Addict In The Family, and Stay Close* all gave me the misconception that no matter how sick the addict was, they lived. Those books will be burned with the next fire.

Where were the books to shatter my illusion? Where were the books to let parents know that addicts die? Addiction is no fairytale. There is no happy ending.

Writing your obituary was brutal. I remember pacing around the kitchen while Ray sat at the computer. I was sobbing and shaking as I tried to find the words to honor your life. A life cut too short by your demons.

We kept the service private. Family and close friends would be the only ones sharing my grief. I feared your drug buddies would come and I couldn't risk the reaction of your brother. I lost one son, I could not lose another.

The day I foolishly thought would never be part of our journey is here. I always thought it would be you and Mike saying a final goodbye to me. Never the other way around.

It's snowing. I run outside and look at the sky. Is that you, Matt? I want to grab each falling flake and hold it to my heart. Matt, how will I survive this day? I stand outside closing my eyes and remember coming home one night crying after losing a baby in the NICU.

"Mom, I don't know how you do that." You gave me a hug and said, "It must be so hard when a baby dies."

Now it's my baby who died. My soul is broken, and I want to stay here watching the flakes fall from the sky, not go to say goodbye.

The day was cloudy and dark. The weather mimicked my soul. Snow continued to fall. I stood in my bedroom staring at the borrowed black dress. My brain not able to allow my heart to feel. I am numb. My body in survival mode. I will need the strength of an army of angels to get through this day.

There is nothing that can be done to ease my pain. I am weighted down by grief. My limbs have turned to lead, my movements slow. I remember once again feeling like an actress getting ready to play a role she didn't want.

My face shows years of stress and days of profound grief. My eyes have no shine. Shark eyes. No life.

I am the walking dead.

I don't waste time with makeup. My tears continue to fall. I remember being in Ray's car. He is driving to our church. The same church we attended together will be the place where we will say our last goodbye.

I walk in alone. I need to prepare myself for this moment. Picture boards are placed next to your urn. I cannot look. I walk to your urn and give you a hug. Sobs rack my body. This is what's left of you, my precious child. Once again it's just you and me. My brain screaming, *this can't be.*

My heart is breaking as the reality of our life washes over me like the waves we used to run through. I close my eyes and we are laughing and running. So full of joy and life. I'm so lost in my fantasy that I don't realize friends have lined up to pay their respects.

I'm hugged over and over. Boys you grew up with now men, telling me how much you were loved. Their parents' shocked faces afraid to look me in the eye. How does a mother bury her child?

The line seemed to go on forever. Muffled voices mixed with tears all coming to show support. I feel like a robot. Shaking hands and allowing people to hug me. The only hug I want to feel is from you.

I've put on my grief mask, pretending to listen to words when all I hear is the roar of the ocean. I've been offered pills to help me get through this. I am angry. I felt the pain of giving you life. I need to feel this pain of saying goodbye.

Finally, the line is over. The service is starting. The songs I chose fill the church with beautiful music, songs you started listening to by Casting Crowns and Mercy Me. The words gave you hope, and increased your faith in Jesus.

I sit between Mike and Ray, holding on for dear life as our minister tearfully talks about your life. He became your friend and tried so hard to help during your dark days. He is overcome with emotion.

Your brother is shaking as tears spill down his face. Oh, God, my boys were supposed to grow old together, hang onto each other when I was gone. Your brother, struggling so hard to be strong, has become a sobbing little boy. His only brother, his partner in crime, now gone.

I don't know how I did it. I'd written another letter to you and wanted it read at your service. It was my final tribute to my son, my hero. You struggled for so long to get clean. Your struggle was now over; mine was just beginning.

I took a deep breath and stood up. I walked to the podium where our pastor was speaking just minutes before. My vision was blurry and my voice cracked with emotion. I held on for dear life as I started to share our story with those who loved you the most.

Dear Matt,

You said this day would never come. You told me you loved me too much and could never hurt me this bad. Yet here we are, gathered today to honor your life. A life cut too short by your demons.

Now I stand here sharing my last words about you with the people who loved you so much. My son was an addict. I am not ashamed. I will shout it from the rooftops—my son was an addict!

Oh, Matt, we were both so foolish to think you had the power to keep that promise. The demons were stronger than both of us. Now you are gone and I am forever broken.

These last seven years have been a horrific struggle. Ray, Mike, and I watched you slowly destroy yourself day by day. There were endless nights of worry and torment, not knowing where you were or if you were alive or dead. Nights when I would call out for help and your brother would drop everything and come. Together Mike, Ray and I would devise our next plan to get you to safety.

I thought bringing you home would save you, where I could watch and protect you from your demons. I am your mother and that's what mothers do.

Oh, Matt, we tried so hard to get you to see that drugs weren't the answer. So many rehabs, programs, and counselors. We thought we were on the right track. Now I stand here and look at your brother's face and realize how foolish we were to think we could outwit the demons.

There were so many times we had hope. Spring came and the old Matt was coming back. You told me you wanted that monkey off your back. A new rehab, the start of a new life. Mike, Ray, and I could only see you on Sunday for one hour due to the rules. I remember us sitting together looking out over the water thinking we finally did it, we beat your demons.

You looked so good. Your face and eyes so clear. You said you were done with drugs and looked so forward to a new life. Nowhere to go, as the demons lived in Delaware.

Your new life in Florida was supposed to be a fresh start from the demons that followed you most of your life. You and I are beach people. We shared a feeling of peace with God by the sea. We talked every day. You told me you loved it near the ocean. You felt so blessed at the chance for a new life. Finally, there was joy, hope, peace and sleep for Mike, Ray and I.

I deceived myself into thinking our nightmare was finally over. Little did I know it was getting ready to destroy us.

The last time we spoke was Friday night, January 2, at 6:23 p.m. You sounded normal. My trained ears heard nothing to prepare me for what was to come. We ended our call as we always did.

"I love you, Matt."

"I love you, Mom. I'll talk to you soon."

That next call never came.

For reasons I will never understand, reasons that will haunt my heart for the rest of my life, you used, overdosed, and was left in a motel room by the man I trusted with your life.

You died at 4:50 a.m. Saturday morning. I remember waking at that exact moment feeling like something was horribly wrong. A cool breath surrounded my body at the same time your spirit was leaving yours. Was that you, Matt, giving me one last hug?

I am so proud of the man you were. You were loving and giving. You, who had nothing, would give it away to someone in need. If you could only read what your friends are posting on your Facebook page. How much you were loved. How you were looked up to and how devastated everyone is by your death. I wish you had loved yourself enough.

I've read that losing a child doesn't just change you, it destroys you. Matt, I am destroyed. Pieces of my shattered heart still beat in my chest, I have become the walking dead. Feeling nothing but the profound sadness that has taken up residence in my soul. I'd gladly ride the rollercoaster of chaos with you again. I would gladly exchange my life for yours. I will never understand.

Your nightmare is over while mine has just begun. I am going through a withdrawal from your addiction. You see, Matt, you were not the only addict in our family. I was addicted to saving you. Now I must find a way to make it through the rest of my life.

I'm told I must go on. My toughest struggles are ahead of me as I navigate this life. Knowing that I will never hear your voice or look into your beautiful eyes again is just too much to bear. There will be no more birthdays, no wedding, no children. Everything is gone with you.

There's a saying that life's a beach. I pray heaven is your beach and you are free, playing in the ocean like you did as a boy. When I can breathe again, I will free you and your beloved dog Kahlua into the sea you both loved so much. Until then, you are coming home with me.

Even though you were a man, you will always be my towheaded beautiful boy. I will love you forever. I pray you will meet me when I take my last breath. Wait for me by the sea we both love. I want to open my eyes and see your handsome face. I want to look into your eyes and know that I am home. I want to grab your hand and run laughing into the surf that we both so love.

Godspeed my precious son. My wingman. Until we meet again.

Love, Mom

Matt Klosowski

Fighting through the fog

Matt,

Today is unbearable. There's nothing left to do. Last week my mind shrouded in grief had to function. I had no choice. First, I had to get you home to Delaware. Flight after flight was canceled because of the snowstorms. I wondered if that was you, your last joke on me.

I remembered how you loved the snow. I close my eyes and see you, me and Mike racing out the door into the newly fallen snow. The dogs on our heels. Boys in the bodies of men squealing with laughter as we slammed each other with snowballs, darting through trees or whatever cover we could find. Not a care in the world. Just a mom and her teenage sons. The age of innocence before any thought of drugs would enter our perfect snow-covered world.

Soaked and exhausted, we would drop to the ground and spread our wings. Snow angels. Three in a row.

Matt, your angel is forever gone. Blown away by the wind of your demons, never to return again.

Writing your obituary and planning your memorial service were the most painful events of my life. Trying to find words to describe your life. What does a mother say about her son's life? How do you describe the towheaded little child who held your heart in his hands? How do you describe the man, the struggle, and the demons?

How do you put the last seven years into a word document when you can't breathe and comprehend that this is reality? You and Mike should be going through this. Not me and Ray. You were supposed to live. You were supposed to be here when I left, to stand by your brother's side and say goodbye to me. Not the other way around.

So now what is left for me? My life revolved around saving you. You are gone and I am left shattered. Like a wine glass thrown against a wall, there is no putting me back together.

I sit alone curled up by the fire. The pups feel my grief. I am dark, unreachable, untouchable, numb. Grief has swallowed me up.

I sit and relive every moment. Memory after memory floods my foggy brain. I dissect every decision made during your addiction and torture myself wondering what I missed. What I should have done differently. I have become my own personal punching bag.

My life now lived in a thick fog. My heart not allowing the truth to find my brain. I don't understand how my heart can hurt so deeply and still beat. Sleep is sporadic. The couch has become my bed. Ray must sleep.

I toss and turn and cry. When sleep comes, it's short and sweet, my reprieve from the reality of your death. Waking is punishment. Every morning my grief lies in wait until I stir. Opening my eyes allows a slice of reality in as I see your smiling face staring back at me. Grief gut-punches. The cold slap of reality.

There are moments when I can briefly forget that you are gone. Moments when my brain protects my heart and I pretend you are busy. You'll call when you can. I allow myself to think you are on the beach enjoying the warmth of the sun while I'm freezing in this cold. Then the wave hits, sucking my breath away, and I crumble like the sandcastles we built by the sea.

My denial is laughing at me. Those books written by parents of addicts, the ones I thought knew what they were talking about. The ones that became my bibles. The ones where their children lived have been transformed to an ashy mess, burned on a dark, grief-filled night. Those books are full of lies. Addiction does not always have a happy ending.

My heart remains shattered with no end in sight. The pain of losing you hurts so much more than the pain of bringing you into this world. At least I knew when that pain ended, I would have a precious baby to hold in my arms. This pain has engulfed my world and will never have an ending.

Memories of your childhood flood my brain. My mind has become a movie projector. Both good and bad flood my brain, taking my breath away.

Humpty Dumpty sat on a wall, Humpty Dumpty ha♦ a great fall.

You and I would laugh dropping to the ground singing that song.

All the king's horses an♦ all the king's men coul♦n't put Humpty back together again.

Call me Humpty. Shattered beyond repair.

Matt's Little League days.

Navigating the Turbulence

Matt,

The day is finally here. The day I looked forward to for months. The day I'd be able to hug you again. To visit your new life. To see your handsome face and that famous grin. I counted down the days for months. The tickets were bought before you left me behind. This trip I looked forward to, now filled with agony and despair.

Counting down the days until February 10. You remember. Ray and I were flying down to Boca to spend the week with you before heading to the Keys. You and I would walk on your beach. I planned on stocking you up before we left, going to the grocery store and buying all your favorites.

Plans forming in my mind. Lunches and dinners together. Seeing where you called home. Meeting your friends. You were going to take us to meet your boss. You were going to show us around Boca. I felt like a kid on Christmas morning. Anticipating how I would feel seeing you in person after six long months.

Now, I'm dreading this trip. I will be going to Boca, but not to see you. This trip has turned into a nightmare. You are no longer there. Your cold body flew home on a snowy January night. Your urn sits on my mantel along with every picture I could copy off your Facebook page. My joy shattered. My original plans blown away on that cold January day.

Ray and I head to the airport. The silence is deafening. There are no words. Nothing can be said to erase this ache in my heart. Tears flow as I try to tell myself to be strong. I need to do this for you. One final act of love. I must retrace your steps. I must hear your story. I must bring home whatever you left behind. It's all I have left of you. The remnants of your life cut short by the disease that killed us both.

The airport is crowded with smiling faces. Families waiting to fly off to warmer climates. I watch and have to fight the screams trying to escape my soul. My brain replays your flight home. The cancellations, the delays, the endless wait to see if that body was really you.

Denial was my savior until I saw you with my own eyes. Your still, cold body. Until I touched your face and ran my fingers through your hair, my fantasy of a mistake allowed me to function.

Our flight is called. We stand in line waiting to board. I feel like I'm being led to a slaughter. People rush past. I'm struggling through the quicksand that surrounds my body. Fighting to put one foot in front of the other to board into the nightmare that has become my life.

We are seated. I'm struggling for air. Ray senses my distress and grabs my hand. In my mind, I'm running up the aisle, screaming to be let off this flight. This is not the way things were supposed to be.

Suddenly we are airborne. My throat is closing, my heart's racing. Ray adjusts the air above my head. Sobs are escaping, racking my body. I dream of disappearing.

Landing in Fort Lauderdale, we're met by friends. Supporting you on your journey, they were the first ones who came running when the news of your death spread.

A cloudless blue sky greets us. The day is sunny and warm. My body is freezing. My swollen eyes are hidden behind dark glasses. Even the warmth of the sun can't penetrate the ice that surrounds my soul.

Foolishly, I allow myself the fantasy that you're waiting for us. I imagine how you would look. I scan the crowd for you. I imagine your face, your smile, the sound of your voice. I crave being wrapped in your hug. Oh, God, please help me walk through this hell that has become my life. Tears run down my face as the overwhelming waves of reality hit me in my gut. You are not here.

The Boca Raton Police Station is located in the heart of Boca. We pull into the parking lot. I feel the grief grabbing my throat. I am silently being strangled. I am telling myself to get out of the car. My legs have turned to rubber as I struggle to move toward the door, the door that will lead me to the truth. The door that contains the information that will yield the final blow to my heart.

We're met by the detective assigned to your case. I find it hard to make eye contact. His eyes, full of pity, were the last to see your lifeless body. His eyes and hands touched you before I knew you were gone. I want to reach out and touch his hand to my face. I want to connect to this man who covered your handsome face in that hotel room.

He shares the facts of your last hours on earth. He tells of your relapse. Your distress. Your being dumped at a hotel by the man who cashed my checks and lied to me about keeping you safe.

I sit there listening and feel a power come into my being. The more I hear, the more I want to know. Grief is replaced with anger. I want to hear the ugly, dirty details of how you were tossed away like a piece of garbage. How instead of getting you to safety, this man disregarded your distress and left you to die. I feel you there. Giving me strength. Pointing me to this new journey. My wingman, now my angel, guiding me along this unfamiliar, jagged, ugly path.

Your possessions are brought into the room. Paper bags marked EVIDENCE hold the last of you. My hand shakes violently as I try to sign the release form, my signature unrecognizable and damp with my tears. There is nothing left to tell.

The sun blinds my swollen eyes. I get into the backseat and hug your clothing to my heart. Sobs come as my dam breaks, my anger replaced with overwhelming pain.

Our next stop is Deerfield Beach. Crossing the bridge from Boca to Deerfield, I hear your voice. You could not hide your excitement. "Mom, I found a job. I'm going to be welding. Got hired on the spot."

I could hear your smile over the phone, the pride returning to your voice. Your excitement found its way to my heart. Oh God, thank you. My prayers answered.

The stopping car brings me back to reality. I take a deep breath and walk into the door of Precision Aluminum. We are greeted by your boss, his face says it all. Still shocked that you are gone. He walks us through the shop and shows us where you spent your days. He tells us what a great guy you were. How you fit right in and felt like one of the family.

He tells us how your death has deeply affected your co-workers. I am numb. I picture you sitting on your bench. You posted pics of you wearing your welding mask, that proud smile spreading across your face, your head wrapped in your trademark bandana. My fantasy is interrupted by his voice.

He takes us outside and shows us your car. He tells us he admired you riding your bike miles to get to work. After riding through several soaking rainstorms, he offered you a car. I remember seeing your first post. Standing in front of this beautiful Camaro, you called her your baby. A sob escapes as I open the door and see your shirt hanging over the back seat, your bandana tied around the mirror. I am no longer in control. The sobs of a wounded animal escape my soul, my brain losing the fight to keep me sane.

Ray leads me to the car. I'm gone. I hold your bandana to my face. Steel and sweat fill my senses. Your smell finds its way to my shattered soul. Your scent so welcome, I clutch all I have left to my heart and try to silence my screams.

We head to the beach you loved, the one you told me so much about. Spending weekends hanging out with friends, swimming in the warm surf. I picture you walking toward me as I walk alone. I need to be where you were. I need to feel the sand you felt and walk into the surf where you played. I need to feel you.

My grief, now as powerful as the surf, begins to pound my brain as it slowly transforms into anger.

I google the address where you lived. I picture myself walking up to the man who tossed you away like a piece of trash. I want him to see my face. I want him to meet your mother in the flesh, the woman who believed his lies and signed the checks. I want to dare him to say the ugly words he spoke as I sobbed. I want him to repeat what he told me when he finally had the balls to respond to my screaming messages. I want him to look at your broken mom and tell me, "People die here every day."

Those words forever branded in my brain. People like you. Those he vowed to help. His so-called clients not worthy of saving. I picture myself squeezing his throat. I want him to know how I feel every day. I want him to experience the terror of not being able to catch his breath. I want to watch the color drain from his face. I want my face to be the last thing he sees as I say your name.

I'm out of control. Ray called ahead, knowing that I am breaking. We are leaving Boca ahead of schedule. I can take no more. We hit the Seven Mile bridge. I open my eyes. I'm surrounded by a turquoise sea. I hold tight to your shirt, roll down my window and drink in the sea air. I am physically broken, mentally spent.

I look ahead at the vastness surrounding me and feel you with me. "Hey Mom, are we there yet?"

You were always in such a hurry to reach our next destination. "Mom, how much longer?"

I see you as a little boy always curious. Your little towhead in my rearview mirror. Oh, Matt, I am so lost. I've no idea where I am going, where my next journey will lead. Right now I need to learn to breathe, to learn to accept the ending to your journey. I close my eyes and hear the gulls crying. I listen and hear your name.

Matt enjoying the beach in Lewes, Delaware.

Lost in paradise

Matt,

We made it to the house we've rented in the Keys. I listen to the excited voices of Ray and our friends. I feel nothing except lost.

It has been one month and eleven days since you left. My life has become a before-and-after movie. I replay the scenes over and over in my mind, searching for that missing piece. Still not able to believe you are gone.

Life before you died was full of hope, promises and joy. Dreams of your future, a wedding, and grandchildren washed away with the outgoing tide. Life now is unbearable. This pain is constant, crushing my shattered heart.

The house is beautiful. The perfect location. I find myself going through the motions of living. I find my mask and secure it to my face, trying desperately to hide my grief.

I listen to Ray and our friends. Smiles and plans of sunshine-filled days. Kayaking and biking. Everything I once loved to do in this beautiful place brings no joy. I am numb. The walking dead.

Sleep continues to elude me. I toss and turn listening to the sounds of the sea. I lay in the dark silently crying. I wonder where you are. I wonder if you know that you're gone. I wonder how I will ever survive the rest of my life.

Days are spent pretending I'm okay. I'm drawn to the back of the house. The turquoise sea surrounds me. The sun kisses my cold skin with warmth. Nothing can penetrate the ice surrounding my soul. I stare out at the beautiful water and remember your smiling face. I look for signs of your presence. I think of this trip, the planning, the joy. The excitement I would feel at seeing you again.

I close my eyes and see us walking together by the sea as we've done so many times before. I feel like I'm trapped in a nightmare. This did not happen. You couldn't be gone. My mind has become an enemy. Never quiet. Always replaying the scenes from our journey. Forcing me to relive every moment, every decision, every fight. I constantly rethink every little thing. Hindsight continues to slap my face. I beg for a redo. I beg to wake up. I beg for this to be a horrible mistake.

I sit in the warmth of the sun thinking of how things should be. You should be spending the day at the beach enjoying your new life, I should be the happiest mom on earth. You told me how blessed you were to be living by the sea. I felt that blessing spread to me, thinking you found your peace and I could finally take a breath.

I try to pray. There's nothing left to pray for. My years of prayers went unanswered. I feel abandoned by God.

I'm surrounded by beauty but all I can think of is you. I stare out at the sea and remember the words that pierced my soul spoken by the man I trusted to keep you safe.

"People die here every day."

Those words run through my head like hot lava spitting from a volcano, smoldering and destroying everything in its way. Were you not a human being? A wonderful man with a horrible disease? A loving son and brother, or were you just a meal ticket for this man who tossed you away? The more I remember those words and his *I coul care less* attitude, his *I'm too busy to talk about Matt* when he finally returned my call, the more I want to scream.

I feel my grief changing. I feel the hopelessness starting to fade. An ember has ignited a raging fire within my soul. Who the hell does he think he is? How can the state of Florida think that running sober living homes like he does is acceptable? What happened to you will never be right with me. Florida, you pissed off the wrong mom.

I first call the Florida Office of the Attorney General. I filed my complaint on the website yet that is not enough. I want to talk to this woman, to tell her what is going on in her state. I want her to know that parasites are making a living off addicts. I want her to know that your mother is outraged and won't accept your death quietly.

My next call is to the Department of Health and Human Services. Next the Governor's office. Your story is being told. Tears and sobs escape with each phone call. They are listening. I feel a strength come over my being. Like you are here rooting me on. I owe this to you. I let you down. I live with regret every day. I had no idea you were flying into a deathtrap when I bought your ticket to Florida.

Now you are gone and I'm left behind. The lone wingman. The one musketeer. You and I had a bond like none other. A bond that even your death cannot sever. Memories of you flood my mind and break my heart. Your laugh, your smile forever tucked safely away in my heart.

My ringing phone brings me back to reality. Your story found its way to FARR, Florida Association of Recovery Residences. They have begun the battle against people like him who prey on those coming to Florida for help. We plan to keep in touch.

Our time here is over and I'm torn. I want to go home and I want to stay. A piece of my heart will remain in Florida. Because of you, I have a permanent bond with this state. There is so much left for me to do. I feel your spirit, your energy by the sea. I close my eyes and see you standing on the beach you loved. One of your last pictures before you died. Joy radiating from your face. Happiness finally found you only to be brutally ripped away. You deserved so much more.

It's cold and gray when we land in Philly. The weather mimics my soul. We pull into the garage. The house is silent. There are no wet noses or wagging tales, no "Hey Mom, welcome home."

Just a dead silence that takes my breath away. I drop my bags on the floor. The memories of another homecoming flood my brain. You were there. The dogs on your heels. Hugs and kisses. Barking and wagging. You were so proud of how you cleaned the house.

I remember your beaming smile, "Mom, everything's done. No dishes or dog hair."

I remember your laugh.

"Bet you're surprised."

The cold slap of reality brings me back. I am home and you are gone.

Leaving a piece of my heart in the sand.

One breath at a time

Matt,

Five months and two days have passed since you left me behind. This is how I count out the days since your death. The days before were filled with periods of uncertainty but also with hope. The roller-coaster ride of your addiction was starting to slow down, allowing me to catch my breath and dream of a peaceful future for both of us.

The years of struggling had taken its toll and we needed a break. I look back now and realize how foolish I was in thinking we had out-smarted your demons. Florida was supposed to be a new beginning, but all we got was an ugly ending.

Spring is finally here. My gardens are coming to life. The days are sunny and warm. I keep hearing that life goes on, that it's been and I should be. No one seems to understand that I am living in an empty shell. My heart remains in pieces. The woman I was died with you that cold January morning. The words still echo in my soul, "It's Matt. He's dead."

That memory stuns my heart and stops me in my tracks. I close my eyes and all I see is your smiling face.

I've read that the loss of a child doesn't just destroy the parent, it demolishes them. My life has suffered from the demolition. I am no longer that smart girl. No longer able to bounce back and be the fixer. I am broken and even I cannot fix myself.

I am no longer that NICU nurse. Nope. I just couldn't put the pieces of myself back together fast enough, so the hospital let me go. Thirty-six years and all I got was a kick out the door. I look back and wish I had spent those weekends and holidays with my family instead of taking care of another family.

How I wish I gave less to my profession and more to my family. We have this false sense that we will always have one more. One more birthday, one more Christmas, one more chance to say, "I love you." How foolish.

So now I'm unemployed. How ironic, I used to dream about the day I could retire. Oh, how I looked forward to having time. No more working weekends or missing holidays. Just precious time all to myself. Time to spend in my life, not running the rat race. Now time has become something I crawl through.

There is a saying that time heals all wounds. People tell you to give it time. Time will help. As if time has the magical power to help you forget your child is gone. All time has done for me is to deepen my pain. Time passes and I realize I haven't heard your voice or seen your face. Time is not my friend. Time is a painful march of birthdays, holidays and special days that are no more.

Time deepens the grief as my reality seeps in and I realize this emptiness will be part of my soul forever. Days have turned to weeks, and weeks to months. Time marches on, and with each day I must learn to survive. Knowing there will be no more phone calls, no visits to see your life in Florida. No Matt coming home for Thanksgiving or Christmas. Time is a painful reminder that there will be no more. A crack that started small is now an abyss that swallowed my soul.

Before your death, I wanted time to slow down. I complained that it was going by too quickly. Days and months were flying by. I wanted time to give me more moments to enjoy life. To enjoy your recovery. To enjoy moments between a mother and her son who survived the ultimate challenge. To enjoy a bit of normal in our chaotic world.

I wanted the change of seasons to last longer, allowing us more time to savor the beauty we missed during your struggle. I wanted to make up for the time we lost fighting your demons. I wanted time to see your beautiful, clear eyes. I wanted time to smell the roses together. To walk by the sea laughing like we had not a care in the world.

Working and fixing you took every second of every day. My mind always on overdrive. Spinning with plan A, B or C. Always trying to be one step in front of your addiction.

Now, time can't move fast enough. I want the holidays to fly away and be gone. Birthdays too. I want time to fly making my head spin away from my reality and the pain it continues to bring. My grief has ended a nursing career that spanned thirty-six years of my life. Time is now something I have plenty of. Something I try to fill every day. The void left by your absence has shattered my very core. Your death hit me like a bucket of ice water. Taking my breath away and putting me into a state of shock.

Time has also taught me a lesson. I have no control over it and what it may bring. We've all heard the saying, "In God's time, not ours." Now, through my grief I understand. Time does not belong to us. Time, however long or short, is a precious gift.

For now, I will use this time to remember you, my beautiful boy. I will let my tears flow at will. I will scream into the wind on a cloudy beach. I will run into the surf, close my eyes and remember.

I will continue to tell your story. I will hold you in my heart forever. I will have conversations with God, asking questions only he can answer. I will use this time to remember my blessings. I will use this gift of time to start healing my heart and soul. This gift of time is a double-edge sword. I have no choice. You are gone and I'm left behind to find my new normal. One step, one day, one breath at a time.

Matt's damn angry mother

Matt,

It's been six months and I'm still trying to breathe. I've been told that by now I should be angry at you. Enough time has passed that the anger should come. The well-publicized stages of grief states that I am in the anger phase. Well, I'm angry. I'm damn angry.

I'm angry at the broken system that let you down. I'm angry that the insurance industry places more value on saving money than saving lives. I'm angry that addiction is discriminated against by both the medical community and the insurance industry.

I'm angry that addiction is not treated like the disease it is. I'm angry at the lawmakers who turn a blind eye to this epidemic, allowing scumbags to run sober living houses, only caring about collecting rent from their tenants and not giving a damn about helping the addict.

I'm angry that lawmakers sat back and allowed relapsing addicts to be thrown into the streets or taken half unconscious to motels where they later died. I'm angry that my handsome, funny, loving son died in a motel room because no one gave a damn.

I'm angry that the healthcare system continues to allow over-prescribing physicians to change everyday people into addicts and destroy their lives.

I'm angry that addiction carries a stigma.

I'm angry that every day I live with the crippling pain knowing that I will never hear your voice or see your smiling face again. I'm heartbroken knowing I will never dance at your wedding or hold your child in my arms. I'm sick that you have been robbed of a beautiful life.

I'm broken when I see the pain on your brother's face and hear his voice crack when he says your name. I'm angry that our lives have been demolished beyond repair.

I'm distressed that most of my friends have disappeared. The ones that remain I can count on one hand. I'm heartbroken that I can no longer spend time with you walking our dogs by the sea we both loved. I'm so damn angry I want to scream.

There are days I get on my bike and ride like the wind, pushing myself to release the pain. Crying, praying, and screaming as I pedal to release this anger everyone thinks should be directed at you. Matt, please know I could never be angry at you. I witnessed your struggle. I felt your pain as we battled your demons together.

I know you fought your best fight. I was there by your side with every relapse, every rehab, every struggle. I know you did your best to fight your demons. I am not angry at you, my son. I'm proud of the man you were, of the battle you fought and the life you tried to live. You will always be my hero. No anger, just overwhelming grief that your life is over.

Now my battle begins as I learn how to use my anger to fight for change. Your struggle gave me the education of a lifetime. Witnessing the roadblocks and living the discrimination that you faced every day gave me knowledge I never wanted to know. It gave me a clear picture of the brokenness of the system in place that was not only responsible for your death, but the death of so many others. My list is long. I've got all the time in the world. You are gone and I must find a new purpose or I will never recover.

Funny, since you've been gone I've become absentminded. I call myself the dumb girl. I laugh and try to explain to strangers that once, a long time ago, I was a smart girl. Then my son died. I'm told it called grief brain and I'm a living example.

I started writing lists of every barrier we encountered during your journey. I was cleaning out my desk and this is what fell to the floor, my thoughts scribbled on a piece of balled-up paper. With this paper came a wave of grief. Seeing my scribble hit me again that this is my reality, this list of wrongs that needed to be made right.

Memories of your struggles sucked the breath out of my lungs and punched me in my gut, a powerful grief punch whenever I relive our past. A single sheet of balled-up paper brought me to my knees. I could feel my anger burning with each sentence I read. So many things that could have saved your life helped end it.

My list . . . .

Pain clinics, and the overprescribing pill-pushers who run them must be regulated and have their prescribing practices monitored. They should face disciplinary action when their patients become addicted, charged with murder when they die.

The medical community needs to be held accountable for their treatment and perception of the addict. Doctors must become experts in addiction and treat it as any other chronic, treatable disease. Addiction needs to become part of the curriculum in medical schools, to help educate new physicians in this misunderstood disease.

Rehab facilities and detox centers must have beds readily available. The window of time is brief when the addict is ready to accept help, precious time must not be wasted.

Insurances must recognize addiction as a disease and extend the allowable time covered in rehab, giving those suffering a fighting chance at recovery.

Matt, my anger will never be aimed at you. You had a disease that should have been treatable, not terminal. Our current model of care allows a stigma to exist against a vulnerable population of people with a horrible disease. My anger has given me new purpose. My anger will help me go on without you. My anger will allow me to step out of my comfort zone and fight for you.

I will say your name. I'll tell our story. I'll show other mothers that there is no shame in addiction. I will join the fight to stop this epidemic from killing the next generation of beautiful people.

My anger will fuel my purpose. You are gone yet you will live on forever through me. As long as I have a breath, it will be yours.

Forever in my heart. Forever in my fight. RIP my beautiful boy, your angry mom's got this.

Matt starting a new life in Boca Raton, Florida.

Matt with his niece Madison on her 2nd birthday.

The first year fog

Matt,

The professionals call it grief brain. I call it being hit in the head by a tornado. I used to call myself a smart girl. Once a capable human being. Able to care for the tiniest, sickest infant. Functioning at my highest capacity. Being a wife. Being your mother and fighting your battle like it was my own. Never missing a beat. Being able to rattle off a diagnosis and calculate complicated drug doses while working.

Today my brain is scrambled like an egg that's been dropped from the counter. My brain in pieces all over the floor, shattered like the town that was once whole but now nonexistent. All I remember is being wrapped in a fog after hearing the words I've dreaded throughout your struggle with addiction. "It's Matt, he's dead."

I remember feeling like my body was no longer attached to my being. I was in another dimension, unable to hear or feel anything. I

45

felt a protective cocoon envelope my soul and I heard the door shut with a slam. My brain protecting itself from what would become my harsh reality.

I feel like I'm walking around in a soft, warm fog. Everything I used to be now a distant memory. I feel safe here. My grief cocoon. Surviving the first year without you has been excruciating. I try to break free of the fog. In my psyche I know I must come to a place in time where I can face reality. I just don't know if I can survive.

I'm told the brain protects us from overwhelming, crippling grief. I say thank God it does. I would've lost my mind months ago if my fog hadn't settled over me like it does over the harbor on a humid night. Protecting my heart from the harsh reality of what has become my life.

My nightmare keeps trying to break through. Reality continues it attempts to seep through my fog like blood soaks through a cloth. My brain continues to resist, knowing I am consumed with disbelief and struggling to accept my new reality.

There are days I feel like I'm losing my mind. Days I just cannot allow myself to believe there will be no more you. I'm having trouble believing I've survived a year without hearing your voice or seeing your smile. I go through the motions of life. I get up and crawl through the grief punches. I put on my mask to face the world yet in my mind I'm gone.

I'm told I made it through all the firsts, like I should be given a purple ribbon and put your loss behind me. It's time to live again. What no one understands is that living is the most painful thing I do.

My grief has become a part of who I am. This first year has been the hardest time of my life. Brief memories find their way through my fog. Memories of us on the beach. Life before your demons took over. Memories of a mother and her son fighting for his life. Those struggles seem like a walk in the park when compared to the reality of my life. I go there briefly knowing that if I stay, I will be lost forever.

Every day is a struggle. I battle my demons now as your demons took you away. The guilt of the what-ifs and should-haves spin out of control threatening to crash into my fog with a blazing light exposing me for who I really am.

Learning how to breathe. Learning how to pretend that I feel. Learning that I must go on without you. I feel like an infant needing to learn how to navigate a new life. A broken mother searching for the pieces of her mind, settling back into the protective fog when grief whips her heart.

I'm told life goes on. I'm told the grief changes. I'm told it gets easier. For now my fog is a welcome place. I'm not ready to see the future without you. My fog wraps me in the warmth of a loving hug. I'll emerge when I'm ready. Until then I will allow my mind and heart to heal at their own pace.

For now, my fog is a where I need to be.

Matt with his brother Mike.

YEAR 2

Letters to Matt

An Easter letter

Matt,

It's been twenty-seven months and thirteen days since you left. Today is Easter. It's also the third Easter since your death. I can tell you that time has not helped my grief.

It's a beautiful summer-like day. I'm sitting on the deck letting the sunshine warm my aching heart. I keep telling myself to be brave. I keep telling myself that I've been here before. I keep trying to convince myself that I survived past Easters without you. My brain is trying yet my heart isn't buying my attempt to be strong.

I woke to birds singing and sun shining. For a brief second I felt joy. I tried to remember the real meaning of this day. Jesus has risen, sinners are saved. I thought I could hold back the tears. And then a memory hits. Walking down the stairs, I could see my two towheaded boys. I could hear the squeals of delight as you two raced downstairs seeking your treasure left by the Easter Bunny. My precious boys, so close in age. Laughing and running inside and out seeking eggs hidden wherever I could find a perfect spot.

My heart so full of joy as you and Mike tried to outdo each other in your race to find the most eggs. Perfect little boy faces smeared with chocolate. I watched as you shared your secrets with big belly laughs and sticky fingers. Each so proud of your stash. Each trying to get your hands on the others candy. Your laughter, so innocent, echoes in my mind. Two boys sharing life as only brothers can, memories and pictures so precious in my heart.

Your last Easter here brought laughter and joy. Your face, now handsome, smeared with chocolate as you tried to convince me that you were too old for a chocolate bunny. Your body now grown, your heart still that of a little boy.

Memories of life before the demons. Joy and laughter. A mother loving every precious moment of life with her sons. Life as it should have been, you married with children. Life where this grieving mother should have been making Easter baskets for your children. A family celebrating tradition of towheaded babies with chocolate-stained faces and sticky hands running into their grandmother's arms. Your children I will never meet. So much loss and pain for your mother to bear.

Today I will allow myself to remember every moment of your life. I will allow tears. I will accept that life will never be the same without you. Memories tucked safely in my heart will bring both joy and pain. Dreams never to be.

Today I will accept that you are safe. Your demons are no longer in control. I will acknowledge that you are with Jesus, celebrating his resurrection in the most beautiful of places. I will give thanks for the years you blessed my life. I will love and remember you forever. Rest in the arms of Jesus. Until we meet again.

A gift from my friend. My prayer is for Matt to be safe and whole in the arms of Jesus.

Grief & *guilt as constant companions*

Matt,

Grief is defined as keen mental suffering over loss. It encompasses sharp sorrow and painful regret. Grief and guilt take turns pounding pain into my heart, each hitting me when I least expect. Sweeping me up in emotions I can no longer control.

I never knew that grief could physically hurt. I never knew that guilt could be so cruel. My body feels beat up. Every muscle and bone feel the pain of loss that no one can see. This incredible anguish cannot be described. I could never imagine that this type of pain existed until it crept into my soul the day you left me behind.

My books on addiction have been replaced by books on grief. Books that no mother should ever have to touch or read. Books on the stages of grief and how to survive each one. Titles lining the shelves that bring tears to my eyes. *The Bereaved Parent, Transcending Loss* and

When A Chil• Dies From Drugs have replaced *Stay Close, An A••ict In The Family* and *Beautiful Boy.*

Those books gave me a false sense that you, like their, children would also survive. Those books met their demise on a snowy, grief-filled night as I tossed each one into my roaring fire. Those books made me feel like I failed to be that perfect parent who did everything right. You know, the parents who can brag that their child beat the demons and now leads a productive life.

My jealousy rears its ugly head and my guilt slaps me like a foul-mouthed child. Where are the books that have our ugly ending? The books that would warn me that endings are not always answers to our prayers. The books warning of middle of the night phone calls that bring parents to their knees.

Guilt then replaces my grief. The what-ifs and should-haves wrap me in a tight cocoon, refusing to let me go. Feelings of failure course through my veins replacing my grief with powerful emotions of hope-lessness and regret.

Flashbacks dance through my brain, things done and said in anger and frustration whirl through my mind. Knowledge I have now that eluded me then. Trying to save you and survive life changed my rational mind into a crazy, calculating one. Your addiction became mine. Staying a step ahead of your demons took every ounce of my being.

Now in a calmer state, I see things clearly. My rational mind sees things I should have seen when I was losing it. I have become someone I do not want to be. My soul caught in a perfect storm, tossed between two painful emotions. Grief and guilt holding hands as they dance over my heart.

Some days weathering the storm is almost impossible. There are days I want the storm surge to carry me out with the tide. To drown my grief in the sea we both so loved. To stop my pain, to sweep me away, allowing my pain to dissipate with the sea spray.

Sadly, I have become a swimmer. I'm the one pulling parents out when they're struggling to stay afloat, fighting the same storm surge that has consumed my soul. Forgetting how soaked I am in my own grief, I throw a life preserver to rescue those drowning in my sea.

Still, there are days when even rescuing another has no impact on my heart. I fall into the abyss of the perfect storm. I wonder why your grip kept slipping from the life preserver I continued to throw in the midst of our storm. Why were you swept so far away from my attempts to save your life? I look at the sea and remember holding tight to your small hand. So tiny yet fitting perfectly in mine. As you grew, your hand became harder to hold, slipping away again and again until you disappeared.

There are days the grief storm is manageable. Putting on storm shutters and hunkering down, I survive. There are days the power of the grief and guilt pulls me into the undertow of reality sucking the breath from my lungs. This sea of grief and guilt everchanging is where I've lived since you left me that cold January day.

I now navigate the powerful waves on a daily basis. Some days the waves hit gently and I can walk through without falling down. Other days a wave hits without warning, knocking me to my knees. Learning to weather the unpredictability of my storm takes practice, self-forgiveness, and patience. Navigating through this storm is tough.

Attempting to hold myself together while I slowly pick up pieces of broken sea glass that used to be my heart.

Matt (age 3) with his brother Mike (age 4).

Anger transforms into advocacy

Matt,

There are days when all I can do is sit and think about your addiction. Days I devour every article I can find, trying to understand what went so horribly wrong. I disassemble your entire journey in my mind trying to find that missing piece that somehow got overlooked during your struggle with addiction.

Since your death, I find myself immersed in your world. I feel like a detective always searching for answers to questions that dance in my brain. Educating myself like I'm about to take the exam of a lifetime and if I fail, I will disappear. Trying to understand the power of cravings and how your prescribed pills changed the chemistry of your brain, changing you into someone I only recognized from the outside. Your looks didn't change. You were still handsome with those eyes that melted my heart. Your changes were in the depths of your soul.

I remember calling your addiction our dirty little secret. I wanted to keep it safe and sound, protecting both of us from the ugliness and stigma that surrounded your misunderstood disease. I remember brief periods of time when we were given a glimpse of normal. Those too-short periods when treatment brought you back from the abyss that had become your life. I think back on the struggle to find that perfect place. The one that would keep you safe and provide me with a much-needed break from the endless worry that danced through my mind.

Watching your struggle taught me that helping an addict is like matching fingerprints. You must continue until that perfect match is found. We were never able to continue, never able to find your perfect match. Too many roadblocks set you up for failure.

People were trusted and money was wasted. I've heard addiction referred to as chasing the scream. My version was chasing the dream. The dream that we would bust through the roadblocks and you would be a survivor. The dream that life would return to normal and your addiction would ride off into the sunset.

That dream now lay shattered at my feet. I am the lone survivor of your addiction. I wanted to deal with my grief and let your addiction become part of my past. I wanted to disappear and lick my wounds, guarding my heart like a mama bear. No more pain for me. I wanted quiet times and precious memories to fill my broken heart.

I thought I could bury the pain with you and move on. What I never understood before your death slapped me in the face and shook me to my core was that once you have witnessed the struggle and have lost your child to this mistreated disease, it becomes a part of who you are. The pain and loss course through your being. Once you live the stigma and witness the hate, addiction becomes inescapable. I was not the addict yet I've learned how society hates those who suffer. I have learned that stigma lives long after the addict dies.

I never planned to become an advocate. I craved some type of normal. For seven years my life was a rollercoaster ride. During that time all I wanted was to get off and find stable ground. Now, that ride has ended and it's the only place I crave to be. I have nothing from the only world I knew. No Matt, no career, just endless time to think about what should have been.

I'll never forget the day my life found a new path. I read an article about a first responder. This man felt using Narcan was a waste of time. He felt addicts should just die. I remember my body starting to shake. My heart beating like a war drum. Anger burning in the depths of my soul. You were one of those people he wanted dead! I was out of control. He never knew you. He had no idea that you were the victim of a pill-mill practice. That by following doctor's orders you became addicted. He had no clue how hard you fought for your life. Yet here he was someone in uniform wanting those suffering from addiction to just die.

With shaking hands, I called his fire chief and then the mayor of his town. I felt a calmness envelope me like you were there wrapping your soul around mine. A sense of peace that I hadn't felt in such a long time. Your spirit was with me on that day. You guided my words and calmed my heart. I told our story. A beautiful man and his grieving mother. The battle for treatment. The struggle for compassion.

I felt that by sharing the reality of your struggle, I could open the eyes of people who have no clue. By sharing the grief of loving then losing you, I could strike back at the stigma that continued to fuel the hate toward your misunderstood disease. My call was met with compassion and concern. A man who understood your mother's grief. The firefighter was relieved of his duties. A victory for all those impacted by addiction.

On that day an ember caught fire. My soul experienced a rebirth. A new passion burning for truth and justice. Staring into the star-filled sky, I could see your smiling face. Your beautiful eyes. The whisper of the icy wind saying your name.

Matt, as long as I live, you live. Forever connected by the bond that even death cannot break. Forever in my heart. Your grieving mom has put on a new hat.

Speaking at the Fed Up rally in Washington, D.C.

Surviving Mother's Day

Matt,

Mother's Day is two days away. I can feel the dread hanging outside my heart like a lost dog crying to be let in. I've fought all week to keep my mind so busy, hoping that I would forget what this Sunday signifies.

I'm fighting for my life. Battling my reality against the fantasy I've created in my mind. I cannot allow myself to believe that you are gone. I must protect my sanity with every ounce of my strength.

In my mind, you are living at the beach. Living life in recovery, working and healthy. My fantasy is where I go when the abyss calls to me. Threatening to take me to a place I cannot allow myself to go. Hanging on like a cat hanging from a tall tree. Knowing that if my grip loosens, I will fall so deeply into grief I may never return.

My survival depends on how long I can pretend. Reality is dark and ugly. My legs push through quicksand, trying to run from what is real. Trying desperately to keep my mind in fantasy mode. Knowing the mask I wear will crack and crumble if reality sinks in.

I tell myself it's just another Sunday. I avoid looking at Mother's Day cards when shopping. I stay as far away as I can from reminders that there will be no more cards signed *Love, Matt.*

This grief can never be described. There are no books instructing me on how to survive a day that brings such incredible pain. A day that even Hallmark cannot put into words.

I plan to run away. Like an angry, unhappy child I am running to find my peace. Our sea beckons me to come, to breathe and remember. I need to be where you were. I need to feel you wrap around me like the ocean breeze. I need to hear the seagulls cry your name. I need to sit and hold onto myself while allowing my mind to go there.

I'll allow myself to remember past Mother's Days spent together by the sea. Sitting close as the sun kissed our skin with warmth. Walking together with the pups, the surf soaking our pants as unexpected waves hit. Laughing as wet, sandy dogs ran barking and biting at the surf spray hitting their noses. A mother and her youngest son spending time together at their peaceful place. A son fighting a horrible disease. A mother who refused to give up.

A mother now grieving your loss. Her heart shattered into a million pieces never to be whole again.

Those days full of hope and dreams. Sun, surf, and a love shared between a mother and her son. You were never too old to say, "I love you, Mom." Never too old for hugs. A little boy in the body of a man. My forever towhead running on the beach squealing with delight as the waves rushed to pull you in. Reaching for me to be your anchor, pulling you safely ashore.

You and I had something special. A truth, an honesty that few shared. I was never afraid to tell you how much you meant to me. How much your addiction changed my life. How badly my heart ached for you and how helpless I felt in your battle.

This Mother's Day, I'll allow bits of reality to find a path through my fantasy. Memories now so painful and precious are what I have left of us. Those precious days we shared by the sea. Like a film projector, I will control how much my heart can handle. I will protect my sanity while allowing those memories to keep you alive. I will look for signs that you are there walking by my side.

I will close my eyes and hear your voice. I will see your smile in the clouds. I will pray that you know I'm here in our special place looking for the missing piece of my heart. Be my anchor, my beautiful boy. I need you to keep me sane.

Until we meet again, I will always look for you.

A Mother's Day gift.

United by addiction, bonded by grief

Matt,

I had the amazing experience of attending the Fed Up rally and Unite to Face Addiction concert in Washington, D.C. this weekend. When I was in the midst of the battle to find you help, I felt so alone. I felt isolated. I felt that no one cared. I had no idea how many other mothers knew my heartbreak.

I was having second thoughts about attending. Every weather report dampened my spirits and made me think of staying home and staying dry. Then I looked at your picture and felt that gut punch of knowing you were really gone. The broken system failed us both and you paid with your life. As I continued to stare into your beautiful eyes, I felt a power in my soul like I'd never experienced before. I had walked through hell during your active addiction, why would I let the threat of heavy rain and wind keep me away?

I read about the rally in the paper. They were asking for stories of recovery and hope. I had written a piece telling our story and included your picture. To my surprise, it was published and I was humbled. I also sent your picture to be included in The Addict's Mom quilt. There was no way I was going to miss seeing your face being remembered at this amazing event.

I took a bus early Saturday morning with a small group from Delaware. We knew each other's grief, each of us losing a child.

Saturday was an emotional day for me. It was the nine-month anniversary of your death and here I was riding a bus in the rain to attend a rally for drug addiction. My tears fell along with the raindrops as I remembered the struggle to find you help.

Unfortunately, Delaware had no rehabs. We have one detox unit that never had any beds when you finally agreed to get clean. I remembered conversations begging your insurance company to approve treatment only to be told that you had no days left. How could they treat your disease like you were not worth the time or money spent to save your life? Never in my wildest dreams did I ever think you would die and I would be on a bus heading to Washington to participate in a march to the White House.

The bus dropped our group off at the hotel. We grabbed our rain gear and headed to the memorial. The sky was gray with a light rain falling mimicking my mood. The closer I got the more I could feel the atmosphere changing. When we reached the mall, I was shocked at the size of the crowd. People just like me. Strangers who knew my grief and walked in my shoes. Strangers whose faces looked just like mine. Shock and disbelief marked us as those left behind. Eyes swollen and empty as we wiped tears away with the sleeve of our shirt.

The stage held a memorial filled with names of those who lost their battle. I was brought to my knees when I saw your name. My precious son surrounded by hundreds of those who like you are gone forever. I felt that too familiar gut punch as my tears started to fall.

I wore your picture on a lanyard around my neck. I grabbed it and started to sob. A complete stranger came and wrapped me in her arms, whispering that she understood my pain. Here we were two mothers, strangers, holding each other up as the rain mixed with our tears. Sharing stories of children lost. I witnessed the kindness of strangers forever bonded by a common grief.

I was waiting outside The Addict's Mom tent. They were preparing to unveil the quilt. I remember the wind blowing and the rain hitting my face. My eyes searching the squares until I saw your face. Your beautiful smile right in the center of this beautiful handmade creation. The sound of a wounded animal came from my lips as I stood letting the rain mix with my tears, hugging myself against the heartbreaking pain.

Arms reached for me. Another mother who got it. We rocked each other in the rain and wind as we shared our heartbreaking grief. Another mother living my life, knowing my pain. Angels walking among the crowd comforting strangers.

We formed groups as we prepared to walk to the White House. I looked around in awe. Thousands of people all here for the same reason. The broken system failed their loved ones.

I was no longer alone.

We marched together. We hugged each other. We shed tears together as we shouted out against a system that must be changed. We were empowered by the numbers. We were heard.

I walked back to the hotel with a couple who lost their son. We now call each other friend. This event formed a bond never to be broken.

Sunday morning came with my familiar face in the mirror. Puffy eyes staring back at me. My face changed by grief. The price of addiction is what I now call my new look. I have forgotten how to smile.

I attended a breakfast in Arlington hosted by The Addict's Mom group. A group no mother wants to belong to, but the circumstances of life have left us no choice. It was emotional to meet all the mothers I have supported and who have supported me on Facebook. These women have walked through the same hell and get it. Again I came face-to-face with the quilt. Your smiling face staring back at me and again another mother held me as I shattered into pieces.

There really are no words to describe Sunday's event. The crowd tripled from Saturday. The weather cold and dreary. I stood on the hill by the monument, in awe at the number of people from all parts of the country coming together to demand better care for the disease of addiction. Many holding pictures and banners with names and dates, all here to honor the one they loved and lost. Those in recovery now celebrating a sober life. Everyone had a story to tell. Strangers sharing their souls with strangers, sharing bonds of love, loss, and hope.

Sunday evening Joe Walsh and his fellow musicians held a concert to honor those lost and those struggling to survive. A tribute to this deadly disease, the crowd came alive. When the music started, the atmosphere became one of happiness and hope. Famous artists coming out and admitting they were once addicts. Speeches by people who care and will fight to make changes.

Hope. I could feel it in the air, at last there was hope. Our new surgeon general gets it. Lawmakers now ready to join our fight providing equal treatment for the disease of addiction. Hope. I stood with a crowd of strangers and danced to the music. Joy I hadn't felt for so long coursed through my soul. We held onto each other when a song hit a nerve and tears returned. We sang out loud. We were empowered. Too many people fighting for the same cause. Everyone lost a loved one. Honoring them by speaking out against the stigma.

I still get chills when I look at my pictures of all the faces lost. Pictures of people coming together and lifting each other up in spirit. Strangers becoming friends. Promises of keeping in touch. Of working together for the greater good. I'm humbled by this experience and know I'll never be the same. I no longer feel alone as I remember the beauty of seeing thousands come together demanding change.

There is a saying that if God closes one door, he opens another. My new door has opened and I know I have thousands of people who are fighting the same fight. I'll be your voice. I'll remember your smiling face on that quilt surrounded by a hundred others. No longer alone but humbled by the compassion of strangers.

Attending The Addict's Mom brunch with a quilt displaying Matt's photo.

Father's Day fantasy

Matt,

Tomorrow is Father's Day. Today my mind is full of what-ifs. What if you found recovery? What if you found the one? What if you married on the beach like we both dreamed you would?

I picture you standing by the crashing waves holding the hands of your bride. Her gown is softly blowing, lifted by the soft sea breeze. You're dressed in khaki pants and a white shirt. Both wearing flipflops. Your sun-kissed face so handsome.

You glance my way as our eyes meet, sharing joy of your recovery. The sun is shining down as you become man and wife. I'm standing by your side. Tears of joy falling from my smiling eyes. The sound of the crashing waves take the place of a band. We dance in the sand to the sound of the gulls laughing as if they know how amazing this day truly is.

I imagine getting that call. I can hear your voice. The joy and fear mingled together as you tell me you are going to be a father. My heart so ready to welcome your child. I close my eyes and remember my little towheaded boy, your crooked smile and silly laugh. I remember your tenderness with animals. Your love for the sea. Your feistiness when trying to keep up with your big brother, Mike. Most of all I remember your beautiful eyes. Indescribable in color. A beautiful contrast to your natural sandy hair.

Memories of your childhood rush through my mind. Losing your first tooth. Your first homerun in Little League. That proud smile as you yelled at me to let you go as I stood back and watched you take off on your first bike. Your tan face shining in the sun as the biggest fish hung from your pole.

I allow myself to imagine you as a father. Meeting you at the hospital as you welcome your first child. I always imagined you with a girl. A sweet towhead like you. A tiny thing you would carry close to your heart. I would watch as you wore your heart on your sleeve as she wrapped you around her finger. I imagine you placing your precious child in my arms as we both cry tears of joy at this miracle of life.

I stare into those amazing eyes just as I did so many years before when you were placed into my arms for the first time. Overwhelming love floods my being as I remember your softness. Your smell.

I imagine her grabbing my finger like you did and holding on as we rock together. I imagine you bringing her to the sea you love. I see the two of you running through the surf with a black lab puppy biting at your feet. Familiar squeals fill the air.

You glance back at me remembering when it was us. A mother and her young son loving the innocence of running through the crashing surf. The dogs barking, the gulls yelling. You are now a man, a father, and my heart is soaring like a kite caught in a beautiful breeze as I watch you.

Reality hits and shatters the beauty of my fantasy. You are gone. You left no one behind. No precious child to help your broken mother survive life without you.

During your active addiction, I was relieved there was no child to witness your struggle. Today my arms ache to hold a piece of you. To hear a voice and see a smile that brings you back to me. To be able to look into those incredible eyes and know you are still with me.

In my heart I pray that heaven is a beach and you are holding a child on your shoulders, looking out at the vastness of the sea remembering me. My beautiful boy, you are loved forever.

Matt with brother Mike, and Mike's daughter, Madison.

Denial is my new best friend

Matt,

Denial is defined as a refusal to accept a past or present reality, a self-defense mechanism that comes from the subconscious mind in an attempt to protect both the psychological and emotional wellbeing of the person struggling to accept the harshness of reality.

Denial is used to protect our minds from a painful reality repressing the truth to guard our mental health. In other words, denial keeps me from losing my mind.

I think my denial started very early in your addiction. Like most parents I just never thought that dirty word would ever come crashing into our perfect family. How could it? I was a nurse. We lived in great neighborhoods and you went to a private school. You went on to trade school. You started a business, lived at the beach. You were living my dream life. How in the hell did addiction creep into our fairytale and shatter it to pieces?

I remember the call. You hurt your back. You needed help. The injury required surgery. You stayed with me for weeks to recover. I drove to the pharmacy and got your prescription filled. Those poison Percocets would one day lead us down the road through hell.

As a nurse, I knew post-op pain was tough. As a nurse, I should have known the dangers of giving you those pills. As a mom, I wanted you to feel better and go back to living your life. Little did I know how much your brain was changing right before my denying eyes.

Denial kept me in that safe place for years. Visiting you at the beach, my denial kept me from clearly seeing the subtle changes in you. The unkept house, the unpaid bills. My denial allowed me to believe everything that came out of your mouth. You worked late. You forgot about deadlines.

"Of course, Mom, I'm fine."

Denial is how I survived those horrific seven years as we rode the rollercoaster of your addiction. Never once did I believe you wouldn't survive. I denied the ugliness as it swirled around our beings. The words spoken, the lies told, the yelling and screaming weren't real. We were both just stressed and so damn tired of how your disease wrapped its chains around us and refused to let go.

I denied that I was an enabler. No way, not me. I'm a mother trying to help her son. I denied that those pills would kill you. After all, they were just pills and they were prescribed over and over again by a doctor! A doctor would never overprescribe and watch his patient self destruct. No way . . .

My denial kept me so protected from our reality. I was wrapped so tightly in my shell, nothing could penetrate unless it hit me like a rock splitting a can wide open. You calling the police after I hid your pills was that first split.

Denial fit perfectly. I could poke my head out for a bit. Deal with what I could and slip easily back into my cocoon. The reality of our lives was harsh. Denial was easy, denial was soft. Denial was my first reaction upon hearing those words I denied would ever come.

"It's Matt. He's dead."

No way. The first reaction was *no!* Matt promised he was okay. He promised me he would never hurt me like this. He promised.

I refused to believe you were gone. Those bastard pills, those f*cking doctors. No, it had to be a mistake. Someone stole your wallet. It's another mother who should be called, not me.

I denied it was you until my cocoon shattered when I saw you laying so still. You, my Matt, were gone. My denial slowly slipped away as I ran my fingers through your hair still soft in death. I laid my head on your chest to hear nothing but the echoes of my sobs.

There are days I allow myself to slip back into my safe world. Days I walk by your urn and tell myself to breathe. Days I deny reality and allow myself the luxury of denial. You're living in Florida. Spending your days by the sea. You're in recovery and very much alive.

Denial is how I get through those days when I feel my mind starting to break. It's how I keep myself from falling into a million pieces and blowing away in the harsh winds of my reality. Denial is a friend

I call upon to survive when survival is nothing I want. Denial is that warm blanket holding my broken pieces together as I learn to live life without you.

Screaming through stages of grief

Matt,

I remember being a nursing student and studying the five stages of grief. The book *On Death & Dying* written by Elisabeth Kübler-Ross became every nurse's bible. I studied each stage trying to understand the power of grief over our hearts and souls.

During my nursing career, I became a witness to the grief experience as I helped many families say goodbye to their loved ones. The echo of screams and uncontrollable sobbing etched themselves forever into my brain. I carried these experiences with me throughout my career. Never once did I ever think I would be the one screaming.

My education consisted of the theory that grief followed a straight path. That we put one foot in front of the other as we climbed the steps from one stage to the next. I always pictured grief as a linear process. We had to pass one stage before we could emotionally handle

81

the next. Textbook grief was so well defined. Like a Lego project, one step built upon the other until you reached the top and returned to the old you.

People were thought to be returning to normal or getting on with life after surviving all the firsts. Grief was supposed to be a temporary place where hearts and souls healed. Grief was like a passing ship. The impact was felt as the wake hit the pier but soon the waters became calm again and supposedly life returned to normal. I always felt grief was like an exam. You had to start with the first question before you could get to the last question.

My grief theory was crushed on a snowy January day. Grief found me. You died and my world came crumbling down. That supposedly predictable and orderly pattern I studied made no sense now that I was the one living it. To be honest, nothing made sense. Thirty months later, nothing makes sense.

Your death has been such a devastating, disorienting time. There are days when I don't know how I will ever reach that final step of acceptance. Really, am I supposed to just accept that your addiction killed you? I'm just supposed to chalk it up to life? I'm just supposed to accept that I can't pick up the phone and hear your voice? Accept that you left without warning? Without a chance to hold you as you took your last breath as I did after you took your first?

I am stuck. Denial and anger hold my hands. They're my constant companions. Denial keeps me somewhat sane. Anger fuels my desire to fight the broken system. The system that let us down and let you die.

I was not prepared for the power of my grief. I was not prepared to become a stranger to who I once was. I was not prepared for the reflection staring back at me when I glance in a mirror. Grief has washed my face and lives in my eyes. Grief doesn't know its stages. It doesn't know that after all the firsts I'm supposed to keep climbing that grief staircase until I get to the top and shout *hoorah, I'm ‹one.* I survived. I made it through and to the top!

My grief is clever. It's tricky. Letting me think that today will be okay. Today I will be normal. Today I will feel joy. Today I will not be carrying its weight on my chest. Today will be better. Today my grief will be predictable.

The reality of my grief is like floating on a tiny raft in a big ocean. Waves hit hard, tossing me in the frigid water. They pull away and allow me to catch my breath before hitting again. My grief has me floating in a fog never knowing when it will sneak up. Grief creeps up and squeezes me from behind as a memory hits or a song plays. I'm dry eyed one minute, a sobbing mess the next.

I have learned in my reality there are no stages of grief. Grief is a crapshoot. It shifts and changes. It's never the same minute to minute, hour to hour. Grief ebbs and flows. Grief has its own mind. It makes you feel like you're losing what's left of your mind. Grief cannot be contained or controlled. Grief has moved into my soul and I have no idea how to evict it.

Grief is as unique as a fingerprint. Grief has no set pattern. However we survive is how we survive. The only thing I've learned for sure is that until you meet grief, you have no imaginable idea of its power over your life. The other thing I know for sure is that grief sucks!!!

 MaryBeth Cichocki
35 mins · 🌐

Proud to be among this group of amazing people.

Activists March On Capitol Hill To Urge Congress To Approve Funding For Opioid...
GETTYIMAGES.COM | PHOTO BY: John Moore

Attending an opioid awareness rally in Washington, D.C. Photo made cover of USA Today.

Encounter with an angel

Matt,

I was having one of those days. The one where grief lays waiting for me to open my eyes before it slams into my heart. The hit is so powerful that I find myself breathless even before my feet hit the floor. Your loss has rocked my world like nothing I could ever have imagined. These days I find myself unsteady. Shaking from the inside of my soul. The ground beneath me is hard to navigate. My journey is one I never saw coming. I have lost my compass, my anchor.

On these days I've learned I must stay active. I must physically challenge my body. I must train my mind to stay away from the reality of my life.

I must keep moving to physically escape the nagging thoughts that constantly take over my brain. I must outrun grief like it's a rabid dog biting at my heels.

This day I ignored the excessive heat warning. Loading my bike on its rack, I could feel the weight of my grief getting ready to follow me on this journey of survival. It was ready to tag along like an unwanted friend as I struggled to find a few moments of peace.

Biking is my therapy. It has become a way to soothe my soul. Feeling the breeze on my face as the scenery changes. Pumping my legs, feeling that adrenaline rush helps push the grief out of my mind.

A bright blue sky with huge puffy clouds greeted me as I headed to my old college town. This town has trails holding memories from a time long ago. A time of innocence and expectation. College life so full of possibilities, hopes and dreams. Biking down these familiar paths brought memories of happy times before life took me to places I never thought I would travel.

I remember biking past Rita's Ice and thinking I should stop. Ignoring my thoughts, I continued on my journey but was unable to outrun that urge to stop. Rita's was considered a treat. I'd always order a mango gelati, savoring every bite. Being out of water and soaked with sweat made the decision a no-brainer. My thoughts turned to how great that gelati would feel sliding down my parched throat.

I found a cool spot in the shade and let my mind wander. Remembering those happy times long ago when I was a carefree student. Wanting a do-over. Dreaming of going back in time, knowing what I know now. Wanting your story to have a different ending. Wanting not to be the grieving mother of a man who lost his battle with addiction. Wanting to leave my grief behind and rekindle the joy that now eluded my life.

I remember the feeling of being watched. I was so lost in my own thoughts I wasn't aware of the couple who decided to join me in my shady paradise. We exchanged smiles and I surprisingly felt a connection. Trying to pretend we weren't glancing in each other's direction, the conversation began.

"Hey, I remember you," this man now moving closer tells me. "You were our nurse in the NICU."

His wife now standing by his side. "Yes, you took care of our daughter."

We shake hands like old friends meeting again. I remember the mother lowering her head and whispering "She was born addicted." We spent weeks in the NICU."

With tear-filled eyes she shared her story of struggling every day to get and stay clean. Sharing her embarrassment that her baby was born addicted. They told me how hard they've worked, both beaming with pride as they spoke of their beautiful, healthy daughter and their journey to recovery.

My eyes filled with tears. I also remembered. Seeing them again filled me with both joy and pain. My grief poured out as I told your story. Sharing your seven-year struggle and your death. Your struggles so similar to theirs yet your ending so different. We hugged, both of them holding onto your broken mother. Tears mingling for a lost life. Sharing a bond beyond explanation.

We parted with a mixture of smiles and tears, connected by love and loss. I began to walk toward my bike still wiping away my tears. I felt a hand on my shoulder. This father built so much like you wrapped me in his arms. I closed my eyes and for a brief moment felt you. I allowed myself to disappear into the comfort of his touch. I drank in the warmth of his big bearhug so much like yours. Memories of how it felt to be wrapped in your arms flooded my broken heart. I wanted to hold on forever. To trick my mind. Never letting you go.

Biking away, I felt peaceful. Like you reached down from heaven and touched my soul. I began to think my stopping had nothing to do with enjoying a gelati. My chance encounter with a couple whose life I touched, both struggling with addiction. A son of another mother. A mother who lost her son. A man who brought you back to me for a moment, this man hiding behind your beautiful angel wings.

No candles, no cake, just heartbreak

Matt,

Today, July 30, is your birthday. It's one of those milestones that we all get teased about. The big four-oh. Forty years ago you came crashing into my world, barely giving me time to breathe let alone make it to the hospital. You had your own timetable and did it your way. Fast and furious with barely a warning that you were making your grand entrance into life.

I remember the first time I saw you. Your tiny perfect face. Those amazing green eyes. Your birth came weeks before I was ready. Your death came just as quickly, leaving me as breathless as your birth.

There'll be no family party celebrating you entering the fortieth decade of life. There will be no teasing about gray hair or the begining of bald spots. No worries about wrinkles or losing your physique. Your brother won't be able to dare you to bend low as you blow out your candles, setting you up for a face full of cake. There will be no laughter, burgers, or beer. The only sound will be in the depths of my soul silently screaming for a redo.

Memories flood my mind of past birthdays. The house full of people and pups celebrating your life. I remember your smile, your contagious laugh. I remember you and Mike sitting around the table thick as thieves sharing stories of your shared escapades, belly laughs over things done and hidden from mom. You never acted your age when you were together. Your personality brought out the child in you both, and I loved sitting back watching my men relive their boyish antics. You and Mike one year and twenty days apart. Both July babes. People called you Irish twins. I called you the loves of my life.

As clearly as I remember the first time I saw you, I also remember the last. Such a contrast in seasons. Your birth a beautiful warm day in July. Your death a bitter cold day in January. I remember hearing your first cries letting the world know you had arrived. I remember the quietness that greeted me in your death. The only sound in the room was the sobbing of my soul as I looked at my sleeping boy, so quiet, so cold. The only similarity in your birth and death was once again it was just us. You and me. A mother and her beautiful boy.

I remember running my fingers through your hair, still soft even in death. There will be no grays for you, my boy, your hair forever light brown. I remember touching your face. Skin smooth and wrinkle free. A hint of the growth you never shaved shadowed your perfect face. Your amazing eyes forever closed. You could not see me standing next to you. You could not hear my voice telling you how much I loved you as I did when we first met. I held your hand and remembered the first time you wrapped your fingers around mine. The times you reached out for me as we ran into the crashing surf. Your hands always reaching for mine. Your hands now so still. You, my beautiful boy, forever frozen in time. Forever thirty-seven.

Today, I will close my eyes and let the memories of you flood my heart. I will remember the joy, the love, and the pain that bonds us forever. I will remember your crazy smile. Your goofy laugh. Your big bearhug. I will picture you and your brother from birthdays long ago. I will remember you crashing into my life on that July night, and I will remember you leaving on that cold January morning. I will pray that you have found peace. I will pray that you are whole in body and mind. I pray that your heaven is a beach and when my time comes, you will be there holding out your hand reaching for mine.

Happy fortieth birthday, my beautiful boy. How I wish you were here.

Matt at his beach house with his pup Beau.

SEPTEMBER 2, 2017

My life before and after

Matt,

I wish I could tell you things are getting better. That after thirty-two months my grief has become manageable. That it no longer holds the power it once did over my heart and mind.

I wish I could say time is helping to lessen your loss. I wish I could lie and say the days of gut-punches, struggling to breathe and the uncontrollable flow of tears after a song, a smell or a memory hit my heart are gone. I wish all those things people say to make things better were true.

The reality is that my life doesn't follow any path or pattern. My reality continues to be one of unexplainable loss and unrelenting grief.

I remember me before the loss of you. A smart girl who loved life. Always finding joy in the little things. Always able to turn lemons into lemonade.

I had a large circle of friends. My home filled with laughter and love. Holidays were full of friends who had no family. The more the merrier. We laughed until our faces hurt and then we laughed some more. Happy hours on the weekends with whoever was in town. Beer and crab. People and pups. Life always full of plans and adventures. Exploring new places in a kayak or on a bike. I was called the clown, the practical joker. Always ready to put myself out there at the drop of a hat. Old pictures show smiling eyes and happiness.

Today, I struggle to find peace. To accept who I have become since you left. Joy is something I briefly remember but no longer feel.

Our house is quiet. Many friends have moved on. I'm no longer that smart girl. Saving babies is a beautiful memory. Holidays once so cherished and looked forward to are now something I fight to struggle through. Once celebrated, now survived.

I never knew the incredible power of grief. I would never believe how it changes who you are from the inside out. I remember holding a screaming mother as she said goodbye to her precious infant. I never in a million years thought I would be that mother screaming for my precious son. Experiencing the heartbreaking loss I witnessed many times in my nursing career.

This grief, so much like childbirth. Until you live it, you can never imagine the pain. My life is in two parts now. I call it the before and the after. I no longer recognize the face that stares back at me from my mirror. Grief has taken its toll. My light is gone. My eyes show a soul that's shattered. I've forgotten how to smile. My laughter is a thing of the past.

I look at pictures taken before you left, and it hits me that in reality we are both gone. Pictures of happiness and joyful occasions. You and me our faces covered in smiles, eyes filled with light and life. From simple everyday stuff like you walking me down the aisle of the tiny church in the woods when you stood by my side as I said, "I do."

Those pictures encompass our before. Bittersweet and what I have left of our life, so precious, so cherished.

Time is now counted out in the months and days since you left. I remember the last conversation. The exact time we spoke. Our last sharing of the words, "I love you."

Before I never counted time. Days, weeks, and months flew by unnoticed. Today every day that passes is a constant reminder of how long it's been since I've heard your voice or seen your face.

I now wear a mask. It protects me from the world. I'm so tired of defending my grief, defending the person I am today. Wearing my mask is easier. I'm protected from a cruel world where grieving has an expiration date. Where grief has overstayed its welcome but refuses to go.

Some days my longing to have you back walks hand-in-hand with my longing to have me back. We left together on the very same day, hours and miles apart.

Matt while living in Boca Raton sober house.

Tug of war with guilt

Matt,

Guilt is defined as a feeling of having done something wrong, a feeling of letting someone down. A painful emotion when one believes that their behavior has affected the outcome of another. Guilt has moved into my psyche and refuses to leave.

During your active addiction, my head was spinning. Taking time to quiet my mind was a luxury I didn't have. Now the quiet is deafening. The quiet has become a powerful enemy. It gives me time to replay every thought, every decision, every move I made to save your life. This unwelcome quiet knows my every move. It lurks ready to pounce when I least expect.

All of a sudden, the lightbulbs that remained dark have illuminated my mind, allowing me to see clearer than ever before. My ah-ha moment. A moment I so desperately needed during your addiction once illusive now smacks me in the face every chance it gets.

I've become a crime scene investigator sifting through the rubble of our shattered lives. Searching for clues as to what went wrong. The belief that I let you down holds tight to my heart. Searching my mind for the actions done and not done that may have changed the outcome.

Yes, I know you were an adult. I hear that voice of reason trying to break through my subconscious when I'm beating myself into the ground. When the guilt joins my grief swallowing me whole and refusing to let me come up for air. I try to remember that you were a man. All my broken heart sees is my little towheaded boy reaching out for a mother who was a thousand miles away.

Mothers are supposed to protect their children. That belief comes with no expiration date. We don't stop loving, protecting or saving when our kids become men. You were so controlled by your addiction you could not save yourself. Being a man really had nothing to do with who was responsible to save you. You were brainwashed into believeing you controlled the disease. You were a victim to a deadly mindset that even a mother's love could not break through.

Now I'm left to sort through endless emotions. To rethink every decision made. To replay and rewind every scene of our very tragic story. The mind is a powerful thing. It has no on/off switch. It has a mind of its own and I have little to no control when the memory will hit, taking my breath with it.

Mothers are born with the guilt gene. I know I was. It came to life as you were placed in my arms and moved into my soul, becoming more powerful each year as I tried to protect you from yourself. I feel like I failed you. I look for signs that you see what I go through.

I question if you understand that you are really gone from this life. I wonder what death was like for you. Did you finally understand that you crossed the line and would not wake up? Did you think of me, or did the euphoria carry you away without a care? Did you picture my face or hear my voice telling you that one day you would forget and fall asleep forever? Did you wonder what your death would do to my life?

So now I fight to survive. I fight to allow a little of my guilt to fall on your shoulders. I fight myself when the full responsibility of your death punches my heart and drops me to my knees. I fight the image of my towheaded innocent son allowing a small slice of our reality to ease my pain. Yes, you were a man with a disease you had no control over. This disease took you away. I try to recall facts, statistics, anything that helps me to understand that I, like you, was powerless over your disease.

I wish you and I could have one last conversation. I wish I could hear you tell me it's not my fault. My heart would love to hear that I am forgiven. That you knew I fought for you and against you to save you. God, how I wish heaven had visiting hours.

Advocating for funds needed to combat the disease of addiction (photo credit: A Butterfly's Journey).

No black or white in addiction

Matt,

Today is my birthday, my third without you. I still have such a hard time believing that there will be no phone call or card signed *Love, Matt*. You won't be hiding in the house to surprise me.

Once again I try to get though another milestone without you. I'm in New York. You know I would have rather spent my day at the beach walking on the sand, listening to the sea birds and the crashing of the ocean. But my article about your addiction was featured in a magazine and I was invited to attend the reveal in New York. This humbling experience was something I could not miss.

Since your death, I have become an advocate for the treatment of addiction. I write and speak about how horribly you were treated by the insurance industry and treatment facilities. I speak out about the ugly stigma that follows addiction. I work to make changes in our state laws. It's the only way I survive.

Your death rocked me to my core. Every day I struggle to find my new normal. Every day I pray that you are finally at peace. Every day I wake to this empty house. My regrets about letting you go to Florida smack me swiftly in the face.

I feel so guilty about your death. I still can't believe I didn't see how wrong it was for you to leave home and go so far away. The thought of you being dumped in a motel to die kills me more and more each day. My guilt beats at my soul. My brain questions what kind of mother lets her son go so far away?

I wanted you to have a fresh start at a new life. I was tricked into believing that new people, places, and things would cure you. All the books written about addiction by people who think they are experts in the field led us down the path of no return. Parents who talk about tough love and disowning their kids because of addiction. So much misinformation published by people who think they have the answers to addiction. Don't they know that every family is different?

There is no black and white, once-size-fits-all in this ugly disease, misleading parents like me that if we follow what they did, our story would have the same happy ending. Looking back, I should have followed my gut. I should have known you would never survive without your family close by to support you when you fell. I knew you better than anyone and still I let you go. Those books have been trashed like they should have been so long ago.

It's ironic. I wrote the truth about us. The ugly, horrible, brutally honest truth about how your addiction stomped our family to death. How your addiction shattered us to the core. How I became addicted to your addiction and turned into a person I no longer recognized. Funny, the editor I sent it to told me it was too ugly to publish. That both you and I were horrible people. That no one would want to read my work.

At first her words crushed me. Then reality hit. The reason this epidemic continues to have such power killing far more than any war or disaster is because many people don't want ugly. They want pretty. People want fairytale endings. They want to think that if we continue to ignore addiction it will go away. That it won't affect our families. That addiction is something that happens to others. That addiction is something we can walk away from and never look back. We only want to hear about beautiful children from perfect families who go on to lead successful lives.

I blame myself. I should have never let you go. I lived the ugliness with you. Yes, there were a few glimpses of pretty, the few times you came back as the Matt I knew. Times when the possibility of our fairy-tale ending played tricks on my mind. Your addiction more powerful than I could have ever imagined. Your addiction won.

Now I live with regret. I live with guilt. The joke was on me. I live knowing that birthdays, holidays, and life in general will never hold the same meaning. Oh, how I wish I read how brutally ugly the true reality of addiction could be.

Matt cooking for housemates at Boca Raton sober house.

Keeping us alive by telling your story

Matt,

Today a news crew is interviewing me about your addiction. I am sharing our story about how horribly you were treated during your struggle. I want the world to know that you did not have to die from this very treatable disease. That had society and the insurance industry felt the need to save you, you would be alive today. But society sees addiction as a dirty disease and feel that those who suffer from it aren't worth saving.

I have a different opinion. You were worth saving. Your life had meaning and value. I remember you before the addiction took control of your brain. Your giving heart. Your beautiful soul.

The problem with society is that people are blinded by the disease. They refuse to see beyond behaviors that are part of the damaged brain. I wonder how many parents would punish their child after a diagnosis of any other disease. Would they disown the child sneaking the candy bar because he doesn't understand the harm of eating it after becoming a diabetic? Why does society feel it's acceptable to label addicts as not worth saving? How can strangers be so harsh in their judgement of people they know nothing about?

After living the nightmare of your addiction, I chose to fight back against a society who has no clue. To honor your life that was cut short because of stigma. I tell your story to whoever will listen. I fight to save other mothers from my grief. I fight to save other children from your fate. I speak out about how you were treated and how society thinks addiction is a dirty disease and those who suffer from it are disposable people.

There is a societal misconception that addiction is self-inflicted. I guess it's easier to form an opinion when you disregard the facts. The brutal reality is that addiction is a manmade disease created by over-prescribing physicians, many who receive kickbacks from the pharmaceutical companies for prescribing opioids for every ache and pain. You followed doctor's orders. You trusted the pill-pushers hiding behind white coats. You became a victim of an industry that cares more about profit than it does for quality of human life.

I guess it's easier for people to point fingers and whisper behind our backs, passing judgement about a disease they know little about. I guess perceptions and preconceived notions are more acceptable when you haven't lived the disease or witnessed the struggle.

I've learned that preconceived notions fuel the stigma and contribute to the bias against this powerful, deadly disease.

I pray that telling your story will begin to break down the walls and change the hearts and minds of those who believe that people like you are disposable. That your life didn't matter. That the disease of addiction wiped away your worth and made your death acceptable to society. I pray that seeing your smiling face and my grieving one will start the crack that begins to unravel misconceptions regarding those who suffer from the disease of addiction. Telling our story keeps you alive. Telling your story keeps me alive.

In Washington, D.C., searching for Matt's name among thousands lost to opioid epidemic.

Justice for my beautiful boy

Matt,

It's been thirty-two months and twenty-seven days since you left my life. Today I'm sitting on a plane heading into my nightmare. My grief hitched a ride on my chest, weighing me down knowing that my trip has nothing to do with joy. This trip is to defend your life. To sit in a room with men who believe it was fine to dump you at a hotel in a compromised state, letting you die alone.

My soul is shaking as we fly closer to the reality that you won't be picking me up as I land. There will be no happy reunion between you and me. No seeing your handsome face or hearing your voice. No bear hugs while I sink into your arms, feeling the warmth of your love wrap itself around my heart.

I am landing in enemy territory. I am trying to keep my warrior mask intact but as we get closer, I can feel the cracks forming as my fear of facing how you died smacks me like a brutal whip. Grief and guilt have settled into my soul once again. The what-ifs and should-haves are dancing in my battered brain. Taunting me with what should have been and what truly is our reality.

I stare out the window into the clouds looking for you. Looking for Jesus. Searching for a sign on how I will survive this part of our journey. I dreamed of returning to Florida. I dreamed of visiting your new life. Seeing you in recovery, living life to the fullest.

I dreamed of walking on the beach side by side as we have so many times in the past. I dreamed of what your future would hold as a husband and then a father. These dreams are now something that will never see reality, scattered like the ashes after a fatal fire in a fast moving wind. I chase after the torn fragments of our life and hold them close to my heart.

Those dreams of what should have been will fuel my fight for justice. I am here breathing where you took your last breath. I am here letting my grief wash over me. I am here gathering the strength to stand up to those who wronged us both.

I am here to defend my precious son. I am here to tell the world your life was worth saving. I'm here to let the world know I will never be silenced.

Let the battle begin

Matt,

The day has finally arrived. The day I've been dreading and wanting to put behind me all mixed into a crazy bag of emotions. My mind is spinning knowing that I'll be facing the men who defend those who feel dumping addicts while under the influence of drugs, who have no sense of the imminent danger of losing their lives, is acceptable. My emotions are on high alert. Fight or flight, hot then shaking, anger then tears anticipating what is to come. I feel like I'm being sent before the firing squad for a crime I did not commit while the criminal pulls the trigger.

I remember hearing the words, "He is here." I felt the bile rise in my throat. I had to stop the urge to run away and vomit. How dare the man who dropped you off in a hotel when you needed help feel the need to sit in a room with your grieving mother!

Walking into the conference room, I felt as if I had walked into a vacuum. I could hear those words over and over again.

"It's Matt. He's dead."

My mind started to scream as the pig smiled my way! I kept telling myself to breathe, just breathe. I couldn't let them know that what I really wanted to do was squeeze the life out of this smiling, arrogant man. I wanted to repeat the words he said to me when he finally found the time to call me days after he knew you were dead.

"People die here every day."

Yes, those were the words that came from the mouth of the man I trusted to keep you safe, who cashed my checks and pretended to give a damn about your recovery. I wanted to watch the color drain from his face as I repeated those ugly words.

"People die here every day."

I wanted to stare into his eyes, knowing that my grieving face would be the last thing he would ever remember.

My fantasy of revenge was short-lived as question after question came flying my way. Some so absurd, I wondered what these lawyers were trying to prove. Ridiculous questions that had nothing to do with the fact that he woke you from a sound sleep and made the decision to dump you knowing you had used and were in a compromised state.

He told your roommate to watch you. Really? A man who professed to be an expert in the field of addiction dumped you off with a kid and told him to watch you? Well, he did. He watched as you died.

As I sat answering those incredibly painful questions, I thought of you. The last conversation we had. The "I love you, Matt," and "I love you, Mom," spun around in my head.

I tried to remember what your voice sounded like. I tried to find strength in knowing that you knew you were loved. Then a flashback to the last time I saw you. My heart broke silently as I remembered you lying so still on a gurney. Your face blue. Forever frozen in time. Forever thirty-seven.

I remember holding onto to you, placing my head on your chest, listening and praying that I would hear your beating heart. I closed my eyes and prayed that this was a nightmare and I would soon wake up.

That familiar gut punch found its way to where I sat. Once again I was being swallowed into my dark abyss. I wanted to disappear.

My tears began to fall. I looked across the table through blurry eyes and wondered how these men would feel if you were their son. Would they be questioning why I am suing this man? Or would they be outraged that he neglected to get their son to a safe place? It's so easy to judge when your life has not been shattered into pieces that no longer fit together. It's easy to sit back and place blame on those who paid the ultimate price for a decision that was not their own.

Hours later we are done. I gathered my strength and look directly into his eyes. I tell him that I will forever blame him for your death. I will forever live knowing that he is a fraud, a liar. His decision that fateful night forever changed our lives. I was never given the chance to hear your voice or tell you I will be there with the first available flight. His decision tore the fabric of our family. You are gone and I am broken. Oh, how I wanted to say so much more. Words are useless to a man who has no conscious or ethics. I decided not to waste my breath.

I found myself on the beach in Boca, the beach you loved. I walked to the spot you stood. Your handsome smiling face, your beautiful eyes captured in a picture days before you left. Your image forever burned into my brain.

I closed my eyes and saw you running in the surf. My towheaded beautiful boy jumping and laughing, reaching your hand toward mine. The wind blew my hair like a gentle kiss from your lips. For a brief second you were there and my heart felt complete. I walked on the sand you walked. I breathed the air you breathed. I prayed for your peace and for strength to continue my fight for you.

As my plane climbed higher into the clouds taking me away from where you last walked the earth, I felt a piece of myself stay behind. Almost as if I was standing by your side on your beach watching as the plane grew smaller and smaller until all that could be seen was a trace of smoke.

A piece of my soul sits and waits for you to come again. To once again walk side by side, hearing the crash of the waves whisper *I love you, Matt.*

This rollercoaster ride called life

Matt,

The reality of your loss sucks. There really is no pretty way to put it. You are dead. The order of my life has been altered beyond repair. Everything has changed. I have a deep pain that can never be fixed. There is nothing that can be done to make this right. Your death was out of order, throwing my life into a place that makes no sense.

I feel like I'm back on that rollercoaster. The one we rode together during your active addiction. One day things were great then the very next moment a sharp turn came out of nowhere, throwing us off course, breathless. I'm a mess. Turned inside out. Struggling to get through the next sharp turn.

This month has been brutal. First, flying to Florida to defend your life. I felt like my already broken heart had been drug over shards of glass, left torn and bleeding in my chest. Being in the place you lived, walking the beach you walked knowing you were gone, hit me with an ugly dose of reality. You really died. You are gone.

The moment you took your last breath, I was counting down the days before I would see you again. All the plans, the things we would do. Lunch together. Walking on your beach. Me getting a glimpse into your new life. Gone with your last breath like a puff of smoke on a windy day. Here for a moment, then gone forever. That rollercoaster once on the upswing, now forever twisting and turning, leaving me unprepared for this gut-punching grief.

My next event where I felt strapped to that horrible coaster was Beau's wedding. Your best friend. The man who sat and sobbed in my kitchen after hearing the news of your death. His tears broke my heart. We shared our grief over your incredible loss. I remember hearing his voice, "I'm getting married."

I want you to be there. Oh, God, that punch hitting again. How can I feel joy for this man who deserves so much happiness when I will never hear those words from you?

I remember feeling that familiar throat tightening as we pulled up to the church. The ride was beginning and I was holding on for dear life. My mind kept telling me that life does go on. This was life and I must participate.

I felt the jolt of the coaster starting upon entering the church. The first twist was seeing Beau. So handsome as he approached holding out his arms to welcome me. The second jolt hit as I felt his arms wrap around me. For a brief second my fantasy won and it was you. The hug my heart craves. I closed my eyes hoping to stop the flow of tears. Reality broke through as the coaster sped up, hurling my heart to the ground. You are gone.

I remained strapped in the mixed emotions of joy and grief. The ride to the reception was filled with small talk. What a nice wedding. How handsome Beau was. How he and his beautiful bride deserved only the best in life.

You were the elephant in the car. Knowing if I spoke your name, my coaster would hurl off the tracks and implode into space. Seeing Beau standing with Mike hurled me into yet another unexpected curve. That twist took my breath away and left me holding onto my sanity. The missing musketeer. You are gone.

My wedding anniversary on the twenty-fifth of October. Married to an incredible man. A man who stood by me as your addiction wove its way through our marriage, pulling us through the hell you lived. This man who never once gave up on either of us. Your crazy mother who was slowly losing her mind fighting to save her addicted son. Or you, the man with the horrible disease. He rode that coaster hanging on for dear life as our world was thrust into the unknown of where the ride would finally end.

This man and our day should have been number one on my mind. Instead all I could think of was you. How handsome you looked. Your incredible smile as you took my hand and walked me down the aisle of our tiny church in the woods. You laughed as you watched the kids on the dance floor. Our picture frozen in time. You walking me into a new life. I stare at us. Both glowing with joy and happiness.

You are gone. We will never walk into a church together again. I will never feel the joy of watching you begin a new life. I will never see you standing next to Mike or Beau as you take a bride.

The rollercoaster of emotions has become my life. One day I think I'll make it. The ride is climbing to a new height. Feeling hopeful that one day this overwhelming pain will start to release its grip on my heart. Just as suddenly an event, memory or smell sends the coaster crashing toward the ground, leaving me holding on, wondering if I will survive this unpredictable ride.

I've always hated rollercoasters. But you knew that. You tricked me into getting on one and cracked up telling me how all you could hear from the ground was me screaming.

Matt, I'm still screaming. Silent screams as a new day begins without you. I scream every day as I try to navigate this life. I scream not knowing where the twists and turns will leave me from one day to the next. I scream your name in my mind as I'm whipped around so many unexpected curves continuously slapped with reality.

You are gone.

Grief doesn't keep track of time

Matt,

Since your death I've found that my grief doesn't keep track of time, people do. I can't tell you how many times I've been made to feel like I am the crazy one. Responses from people I hardly know continue to astound me. I can feel my soul start to cringe as soon as I hear, "Well it's been _____, you should be _____."

On bad days I just want to slap the shit right out of them. I want them to feel my grief physically as I feel it every day. I just can't understand how society thinks that grief has a timeframe. What is it about grieving people that scares others away? Grief is not a disease. Grief is not catchy yet people continue to think that grief is supposed to ease up and then ride off into the sunset. Like grief has a timetable and an automatic shut-off switch. Like grief is some sort of mental disorder that should be over and done with in a specific time period.

The problem with grief is it's tricky. It finds you in unexpected moments. On days I think I'm doing okay, it finds me. Days when I fool myself into thinking that society is right. That it's been and I should be. During yoga class or lunch with a friend it attacks unexpectedly. The reality that I'll never be the old me again, and no matter how hard I try to put up a fight, grief always wins. Grief is a monkey on my back that hides, waiting to show me who is in control.

People think that when you grieve there is something wrong with you. Especially if your grief lasts longer than many think it should. It's like that acceptable timeframe for dating again after a divorce, grief is supposed to be short-lived. After all, we all know life goes on.

I get so tired of feeling like there's something wrong with me, like I'm failing to follow those ridiculous stages of grief made famous by Dr. Elisabeth Kübler-Ross. I studied them in nursing school and bought into her thinking until grief slapped me to the ground with an unimaginable force I'd never known before your death. Dr. Kübler-Ross even acknowledged before her own death that grief follows no path of rhyme or reason. Grief ebbs, flows, and shatters as it pleases.

I've learned that grief is selfish. It doesn't allow me to think of anything other than my own deep pain. It's like addiction. It changed my brain. I think differently. I act differently. Somedays I really don't care what people think. I'm struggling to survive this quicksand that surrounds every step I take.

I get tired of defending my grief. For God's sake, I lost my son. How do I get over that? How does a mother get over saying goodbye to her precious child? Age doesn't matter—we aren't supposed to bury our children. Yet, society continues to think that child loss is something to put away. That we can box up our grief and put it on a closet shelf like old family albums. That grief is something to be controlled.

I am mentally exhausted having to explain over and over again how losing you has shattered the fabric of my life. I try to relate my grief to childbirth. I can tell you how painful it is but until you experience it personally, there is no way you could ever understand how intense the pain can be. How this pain takes you away from reality and you scream thinking you will never survive. This is my grief. Silent screams every day. Screams as I wake and realize that another day is added to the tally of the days since you took your last breaths. Screams as I look at your smiling face in pictures frozen in time. Screams as I attend weddings and baby showers knowing they will never be for you. Screams as I try to be normal as expected by society. Screams as I tell your story to faces who have no clue.

I remember when people were afraid to mention the word cancer. It became the big C. It's the same thing with grief. Is it becoming the big G? Our culture sees grief as a mess that needs to be cleaned up. I see grief as something that now lives inside my soul.

Grief is not a problem to be solved. Grieving people are not to be shamed, dismissed or judged. Grieving is what mothers do when the natural order of their lives has been altered with the death of their child. I never wanted to know grief as intimately as I do. I never wanted to experience grief brain or constantly question my sanity. I wanted you to live a beautiful life. I wanted to meet your wife and rock your babies. I wanted a reality that wasn't to be.

I know I will never return to the person I once was. Going back to that person is not an option. She vanished when you did. Gone with your last breath. My grief path is my own. It's rocky and full of broken glass. I tread lightly on days I can. I crawl through the glass on days when the pain kills and I question my survival. My grief has no finish line. It's one day, one breath, one scream at a time.

My grief is the best I can do. Navigating this path is the most painful thing I've ever had to do. One thing I know for sure is, I'm not okay. I will never be okay. And for me, that just has to be okay.

Don't mind the elephant, he's with me

Matt,

I remember during your active addiction you talked about your disease as if it were a monkey on your back. Since your death, I seem to have inherited an elephant. The only difference is my elephant found a spot on my chest where he decided to settle in.

The funny thing is, as heavy as my elephant is to carry, he seems to be invisible to everyone but me. I first realized how easy it was to ignore my elephant when most of my so-called friends seemed to disappear. It seemed it was easier to just vanish from my life than to acknowledge the tragedy of your loss. For many, my elephant can be a scary beast representing a difficult situation or an unpleasant experience that is best left unspoken. The mentality seems to be that if something is not said then it never really happened. Unfortunately for me, my elephant has become a constant companion. A constant reminder that life has taken a tragic turn and will never be reset.

The elephant is my dirty little secret. My elephant has a name. I call him Grief. I've lived with him for thirty-five months and twenty-six days. Some days he seems to weigh a little less. On those days I seem to be able to carry him easily. The difficult thing is I never know how heavy or how light he will become from day to day. After living with Grief, I've learned that until people inherit my elephant, they really don't want to know how heavy he can be. Some give me the impression that they really don't care.

It seems that my elephant chases people away. While shopping I run into old friends from my past. They know my story yet rather than approach me and start a conversation, they go out of their way to avoid me. My elephant isn't ugly. He doesn't bite. He isn't threatening. He is happy when people acknowledge him, confused and hurt when they avoid him.

I have learned to live with my elephant. It seems I had no choice. Never in a million years did I think my constant companion would control so much of how I think and feel. Even in my wildest dreams I couldn't even come close to understanding the power of one of the gentlest creatures on earth.

Some days my elephant makes me feel like I'm crazy. Like we are too attached. Like I should be giving him walking papers and send him on his way. My mind thinks I've had him far too long yet my heart just can't let him go. The elephant has become emotionally protective of me. Shielding me from those who don't know a thing about elephants, from those who feel that elephants have no place in the human heart.

It seems as though this time of the year my elephant has gained some weight. As I see families huddling together near Christmas lights or hear the songs of peace and joy, I can feel his weight shift. I feel like the loner in the room. Like my elephant has become unruly and people must run for their safety. People see me but don't see me. My elephant and I are invisible. As if someone had the nerve to ask how I was doing, the elephant would shatter to the floor.

I wait for the day my elephant is accepted. I wait for the day people reach out and touch him. My elephant has become a part of who I've become since your death. He needs to be acknowledged. He needs to be understood. The elephant has no plans to move on. I'm still grieving and probably will be for the rest of my days. My elephant and I will leave this life as one.

Until then, I carry him wherever I go.

Matt with his dogs at home on the beach in Lewes, Delaware.

Hanging on by a Christmas thread

Matt,

December 3 marked the thirty-fifth month since your death.

Thirty-five months.

I still can't believe you are really gone. I heard the second year was tougher than the first. Never in a million years could I ever allow my mind to believe it to be true. It seems as though the protective fog has blown out to sea, leaving me a clear view of the empty shoreline.

This second year has beat me to the ground. My cocoon shredded and blown away with the wind. My mind reminds me daily that you are dead. I feel naked, stripped of the protection that the shock of grief provided during those first months when my mind was in complete denial. Grief protects you from reality. The brain builds that impenetrable wall able to withstand the assault of reality.

The second year, cracks begin to form and the wall slowly begins to crumble at your feet. Leaving you with a clear view of life.

Last year I was numb. Able to go through the motions of life. My holiday mask was intact and firmly secured to my face as I navigated my way through the usual festivities. My mind allowed me the fantasy that you were alive, living in Florida. My mind allowed my heart to stay on track, providing multiple distractions keeping the grief under wraps in public.

This year, I've found the mask has dissolved from the flow of my tears. This year my grief has gained power. This year my grief doesn't seem to care that this is the happiest time of the year.

Your loss continues to stun me. I'm shocked when reality slaps me with the knowledge that you won't be coming home for Christmas when I hear that holiday song. Reality grabs my heart and causes me to forget to breathe.

I was told in time I would get angry. I'M ANGRY. I'm angry at our reality. I'm angry at happy strangers shopping with a spring in their step and joy on their faces. I'm angry that my grief continues to hurt so deeply. I'm angry that I've just survived Thanksgiving and now Christmas is being shoved down my throat. Not everyone is merrily anticipating holiday traditions. For some of us, our holidays will never be the same. I'm angry that the woman I see in the mirror is not who I used to be.

This second year has a power I could never have anticipated. My mind, now clear from the fog, vividly remembers painful events. My guilt has returned full force. My double whammy. Grief and guilt have renewed their friendship, bullying me every chance they get.

My mind remembers things it buried to protect my shattered heart. Things said and done during your addiction. The should-haves or could-haves haunt me like ghosts from Christmas past. I look at family pictures. You and Mike on Santa's lap. Childhood innocence, a time of joy and anticipation of things to come. Never did I see this coming. Never did I ever think my youngest son would be gone in the blink of an eye.

I hear strangers stating what they want for Christmas. Children rattle off a list of toys. Adults want more money, a better job or world peace. I cringe and feel the tears start to form. The song, "All I Want For Christmas Is You," starts playing in my head.

I close my eyes squeezing as hard as I can. Trying desperately to balance myself on the edge of my abyss.

I want a visit from the ghost of Christmas past. I want to see my boys squeal with delight as they rip into beautifully wrapped gifts. I want to hear the laughter of two boys comparing superhero capes. I want to feel the joy and completeness of having my family intact. I want to travel back in time before you became adults. Before your injury led you down the path of no return. I want to fix what is broken. I want to close my eyes and see you walk in my door. I want to hear "Hey, Mom, merry Christmas," as your wife and kids wrap me in a big hug. I want to see you and Mike standing side by side belly laughing as a childhood memory cracks you up. I want every chair at the table full. I want to raise a glass and toast to a future full of possibilities.

Unfortunately, *A Christmas Carol* is just that, a fantasy script written long ago addressing second chances. Our reality is a painful reminder that death doesn't give a redo. There'll be no second chances for us. No more watching you and Mike standing together surrounded by your family. No more holiday pictures full of smiles and joy. No more hearing a Christmas song without the punch of grief taking my breath away.

This year when everyone else is dreaming of a white Christmas, I'll be dreaming of the family we used to be.

So, this is Christmas

Matt,

You remember my favorite Christmas song, John Lennon's "So This Is Christmas."

Those words always made me stop and think about what I had done with the gift of the year I'd been given. I would examine my behavior and think about the things I did, and all the other things I wanted to do but put on the backburner for another time. Always under the incredibly naïve assumption that I was in control and there would always be more time.

I heard the song on Pandora today and I had to sit and catch my breath. Thinking back to another year leading up to Christmas without you. So, this is Christmas and what have I done? Another year older and a new one just begun. This year those words hit me as I felt that now familiar wave of grief slap against my hurting heart.

This year I became older but you remained thirty-seven. This year I lived with a grief so powerful, many times I had to force myself to breathe. This year as I looked back, my soul fills with regret. Things I wanted to do with you and say to you left undone. Thoughts that there would always be a tomorrow dance through my brain. There will be no new year for us. No, my sweet boy. No happy Christmas. No happy new year.

So, this is Christmas and what have I learned?

I've learned the pain of losing a child crushes your soul, changing you from the very core of your being. The loss is indescribable, heart obliterating, life-altering. The pain lives in every breath and step I take. This pain is invisible to others yet excruciating to me. This pain has become a part of who I am. It will remain an ever-present ache with every passing moment until my last breath.

I've learned that grief has no stages. Grief has a mind of its own. Hitting so powerfully at unexpected times. There is no rhyme, reason or warning as to when and where it will strike. I've learned not to fight when those waves hit. I've learned to let grief wash over my soul until it recedes. I've learned grief doesn't keep track of how long it's been.

I've learned how brutal the second year truly is when the fog has lifted and reality comes home to stay. Never believing that any pain could be worse than that heartbreak of all the firsts. The second has been brutal. Kicking me to the curb slicing open my broken heart with every memory of a life that used to be. Leaving my heart battered and bloody. I've learned that shock never subsides. I'm shocked with every punch of reality. You are really gone. There is no pretending this year.

My heart knows you will never be home for Christmas. As the holidays approach, pieces of me shatter to the ground.

I've learned that normal died the day you did, leaving me alone to navigate life as a bereaved parent. For the rest of my life, I have to learn how to survive the pain. This excruciating torture cannot be described in human language. My grief overshadows joyful moments as I realize our life is permanently divided into before and after your death. How I think and feel have been severely altered. I have been taught the ultimate lesson. We are promised nothing. Not tomorrow, not months, nothing.

I no longer sweat small stuff. I've learned to hide behind my mask and move on, accepting that people are uncomfortable with grief. I carry my elephant and play the game of surviving around those who could never imagine life after child loss. I've learned that expectations lead to further heartbreak.

So, this is Christmas and what have I done?

Since your death, I have lived the experience of God's power in my life. He closed the door of your addiction and opened a door of understanding and compassion for others. Out of my brokenness, A Hug From Matt was born. Your life taught me to see past the shell of a person by being able to look into their soul. I honor your life by ministering to those who are addicted and homeless. I feel your presence in their smiles and hugs. Bringing joy to those the world forgot brings peace and joy to my heart.

I've found the words to share our story with the world. To shatter the ugly stigma that follows those who suffer from your disease. Words that touch another parent's heart. Words that bring help and hope to those who share our story. From my grief a new person has emerged. I am fearless. An advocate for change in the treatment of addiction.

I have surrounded myself with parents who get it. The broken ones. Parents who were once strangers now hold a piece of my heart. We encourage each other and cry together as we crawl through the days many would never survive. Knowing that until one experiences this loss, it is almost impossible to express. We have a permanent bond. The bond that only a bereaved parent would understand.

Your death has impacted my life in ways I could never imagine. Time now allows me to stop and smell those roses I once ran by. My faith is deeper. Prayers are no longer recited from memory, instead they come directly from my heart. I appreciate every moment I spend with those I love. I take nothing for granted, knowing that in one breath the world can be changed forever.

So, this is Christmas. Another without you. This year I can reflect on the beauty that came out of the ugliness of your untimely death. I can reflect on what I have done to honor your life. This Christmas I will remember your smile. I will feel you in the hug from your brother. This Christmas you will live on through me forever.

YEAR 3

Letters to Matt

Grief, the gift that keeps on giving

Matt,

Today, January 3, marks the third year since you left me behind. Three years have passed since I've heard your voice or seen your handsome face. Three years. It just doesn't seem real. How did I survive three years of carrying the unbearable weight of my grief? I sit alone and remember the moment I learned you were gone.

Three years ago, January 3, was a Saturday. It was snowing here and all I could think about was how lucky you were to be spending your day at the beach. I was working in the NICU, feeling jealous of your new life in sunny Florida. Jealous that I was freezing and you were laying in the warm sun. Little did I know you were already lying in a morgue, your body lifeless, cold and blue.

For three years I've lived in a fog. Disbelief allowed me to survive days when I pretended you were lying on that beach being warmed by the Florida sun. Then there were days when reality snuck in and I had to crawl through choking quicksand. Days when the weight of my grief literally had me fighting for my own life.

As a nurse, I read about how debilitating complicated grief could be. I learned how destructive this type of grief could be to the body and soul. Never quite understanding its incredible power until I was thrown into the fire after your untimely death.

You see, Matt, my grief has been complicated by guilt. For three years I've blamed myself for your death. I became my own punching bag. Constantly allowing that rollercoaster of emotions to chip away at my very soul.

I blamed myself for not being the best mother. For working while you were young, not having the luxury of being one of those incredible moms who had time to make meals from scratch. You know, those moms who never had to be responsible for anything else except their kids. My beatings continued as I rehashed everything I should have done to save you from your addiction. My guilt would never allow me to see everything that I did do. Guilt is ugly. Guilt only let me see all the wrongs and none of the rights.

I remember watching you withdraw from your opioids. I watched your body shake, sweat, and fall apart. I watched in horror, never quite understanding how your body could withstand the assault.

Now it's my body that's being assaulted. I'm the one withdrawing from you. I was addicted to your addiction. For seven years, I fought to save you. Never once thinking that I had no control of our fate. I was so foolish thinking I was in control of anything, especially your addiction. Call it nurses mentality. Nurses save and your mom was a nurse. I spent my life saving people and could not accept that this wonder woman of a nurse could not save her own son.

So now it's me that's been shaking, sweating and falling apart. For most of the past three years my soul has lived in a constant state of high anxiety. Your death caused a permanent withdrawal that I now have to navigate my way through. Panic attacks, ER trips thinking I'm having a heart attack, and my new friend migraines. Every crazy symptom all anxiety and guilt related.

I remember being told that one day I would get angry. Angry at you for causing such profound grief. For causing my world to spin off its axis. For causing me to drown in this dark, ugly abyss. This over-whelming ocean of heartbreak, constantly fighting the powerful undertow that drags me down on the bad days.

I never did get angry. I forgave you the moment you left. The person I need to forgive is me. Three years is a long time to fight the most powerful of emotions. Three years of blaming myself for some-thing I couldn't control. Three years of near drownings when the guilt pulled me far away from my safe shore.

I will grieve and miss you forever. This isn't how our story was supposed to end. I now realize that when the guilt starts dragging me under, I must reach for a life preserver. I must focus on getting back to shore. I must learn to swim again.

Matt with his grandmother at a family party.

Baby steps & hiding behind masks

Matt,

We have hit the three-year mark. Actually, it's three years and twenty-four days. That's how life is for me now. It's become a count down to how long it's been since your death. When my brain realizes how long it's been, I find myself breathless. Still shocky, still unsteady. Unlike public perception, times does not heal this wound.

January's slap was extra harsh this year. Not only was I trying to survive the anniversary of your death, but Ray's father was dying. I sat at his bedside on your anniversary holding his hand. I told him it was okay if he needed to go on your day. I asked him to give you a hug and tell you how much you are loved and missed.

I sat watching the life leave his body but my heart was thinking of you. I was thinking of what it must have been like for you. No family at your bedside. No one holding your hand, telling you how much you were loved. How your life was well lived and there should be no regrets. You see, Matt, that's the hardest part for me. Knowing that as you were taking your last breath, I was a thousand miles away totally unaware that you were gone.

Grief enveloped our home. Me continuing to grieve you, Ray just beginning to grieve for his dad. I recognized that wave hitting Ray, seeing his face change as reality hit his heart. Seeing him in pain filled me with shame. I wanted to comfort him. I wanted to be who I needed to be to support him through his loss. I was barely surviving falling into the abyss that threatened my mind. How could I not think of the three years since I heard your voice?

Fifty years separated your deaths. Your life cut short at thirty-seven. Ray's dad living to be eighty-seven. You see, Matt, all I could think of was how many years we never had. Your death was out of the natural order of how things are supposed to be. Ray was experiencing death as it is supposed to be. People grow old and then they die. We bury our parents. We don't bury our children.

Planning a funeral sucks. The painful ritual becomes unbearable when wounds are reopened. Watching Ray was like watching the re-run of a bad movie. Memories of everything I crawled through being brought back to life. Obituaries. Pictures of happy times.

Torture. Torture. Torture.

I found myself reliving those first days. The days when I survived one minute at a time. Those first days when baby steps were the best I could do. Dressing for this funeral brought back dressing for yours.

I dreaded the funeral scene, shocked at how strong memories can hit. Closing my eyes, I relived every moment. Feelings I'd been able to suppress flooded my heart. The profound loss. The ugly reality of death. I was helpless to help anyone but myself. My mask broken beyond repair.

Rays father's funeral remains a blur. Memories of hugs, smells, and whispers. The cold January wind once again slapping my face with the ugly reality of loss. Bone-chilling cold reminding my heart that three years ago to the day I said goodbye to you, my beautiful boy.

Watching Ray, I must admit I am jealous. His life returning to normal. Back to work. Back to life. Oh, how I wish my grief would allow my life to stabilize. To allow me to have a day when I don't think of you. When I don't think of what life could have been had you survived your addiction.

I understand our losses are different. My heart is still shattered by your death. It will always hold evidence of a deep, painful, unimagineable loss. It will always dream of the what-ifs, the possibilities of having you here. Child loss is the most devastating grief known to man. It never leaves and strikes at the most unexpected times.

Losing a child is losing yourself. The present and future are both tainted with profound confusion and denial.

I've heard it said that grief is not a life sentence, it's a life passage. I thought long and hard about that statement. I think about this every time my phone rings and I hear an unfamiliar voice asking for me. I hear the choking tears as another mother calls my name. Oh, this grief of child loss is a life sentence. One with no stages or reprieve. One we must take in slowly. One we crawl through every day for the rest of our lives.

Grief lives in paradise

Matt,

It's February. You remember that first year when you were living in Florida? February was the month I planned to come for a visit. I anticipated seeing you again after six long months of nothing but phone conversations.

I imagined how it would feel to see you in person. To be able to touch you again. To feel your hug and see your incredible smile. I was excited to see you in a new life. To see you living on your own in the place you loved the most. I envisioned us walking together on your beach and making plans for a beautiful future.

As you know, my dream was shattered by your unexpected death in January. So here we are. The third February since your death. I've returned to Florida. To the Keys. My piece of heaven on earth. You see, that was the original plan before your death. I was spending that first week with you in Boca, then heading for the Keys. You were planning to come for a long weekend. Once again I anticipated showing you my paradise. I planned on how amazing it would be to show you what draws me back year after year. The turquoise water. The cry of the seabirds. The vastness of the sea that surrounds the house. This is my heaven on earth.

You never made it. So now my paradise is bittersweet.

I remember boarding the plane. It was an early flight. I remember just closing my eyes and closing off the world as my earbuds blocked out the noise. I started to pray the serenity prayer. Please God, help me to accept the things I cannot change. You see, Matt, no matter how many times I say that prayer, I will never accept that you are gone.

I'm hanging in until I feel the plane start to descend. Looking out the window, I see the blue water surrounded by a scattering of homes. I hear the pilot welcoming us to Florida, the state you took your last breath. I feel the slap of grief. That familiar throat tightening. I'm choking. The grief lives in Florida. I stare out the window hiding my flow of tears. Hugging myself to stop the sobs that are escaping from my broken soul.

My therapist says that the body remembers. Matt, my body is remembering and physically reacting to your loss.

The airport is full of happy people. Families reunited. I see a young man walk into the arms of his mother. I allow myself the fantasy that you are here waiting for us. I see your smiling face. I hear your *Hey, Mom.* I look for you everywhere. I hide my tears and tell myself to breathe.

Grabbing my luggage, I walk outside into the welcome heat and sun. Ray grabs my hand knowing I need to get my bearings, that I need to allow the grief to envelope me until I can breathe again.

We reach the rental car. The radio starts to play, Guns and Roses singing "Paradise City" fills the air. Oh, Matt, are you here? Guns and Roses, your favorite band, singing about paradise. My tears start to flow. Ray grabs my hand. Smiling, he tells me it's Matt.

The drive to the Keys is indescribable. The salt air hitting my face. The bridges surrounded by the most beautiful turquoise water. The cry of the seabirds welcoming me back. I'm surrounded by paradise as my thoughts turn to you.

Once again I look for signs that you're here. I wonder if you know I'm back. I talk to you as if you are walking beside me, listening for your voice in the sound of the wind. I remember all the plans we made. Plans that have now become a grieving mother's fantasy.

Reminders of you are everywhere. I see you in my mind as two little boys ride skateboards down the street. I see you standing on yours next to your brother with that famous *I can ɗo it, Mom* smile on your little face. I see you in the man carrying his child on his shoulders. I see you in the stars shining in the night sky.

It is said that grief is a journey, that in time the pain will lessen. I'm finding that this journey is an endless path that neither time nor place can soften. Even returning to paradise has become bittersweet. Tomorrow I head home. Leaving both my paradise and a piece of my heart behind.

Matt on my wedding day, October 2008.

Why is grief so complicated?

Matt,

This complicated grief is nothing like the grief people who have never experienced think it is. Most people, at least some of the people I've come in contact with, still think grief has a timeframe. Supposedly, normal grief is still thought of as something you glide through, going from one stage to the next until you reach the finish line. After that so-called specific acceptable timeframe, the grief just disappears into thin air. Like magic, poof, it's gone. Life then supposedly returns to normal.

Unlike the so-called normal grief, complicated grief doesn't seem to follow a timeline. It doesn't seem to care that it's been years. It seems that time can continue to pass and complicated grief just clings tightly to your heart. Complicated grief is usually associated with the loss of a child. This grief is unbearably devastating.

I find that what makes this grief so tough is that you have to constantly defend it. People will bring up how long it's been. Oh yes, believe me, I know how long it's been. So does every other parent who has lived through the death of their child. What I don't understand is why how long it's been should have any impact on how long or how deep a parent continues to grieve.

The loss of a child goes against Mother Nature. Parents aren't supposed to bury their children. The loss of a child shatters the foundation of what we have been taught to be normal in our world.

The loss of a child rocks parents to the core. We begin to question everything we have learned throughout our lifetime. We question our faith. We wonder how a loving God could have allowed our child to die. I remember my daily prayers. Every morning and night I prayed to God for your safety. I prayed for you to have the strength to beat your addiction. I truly believed that if I let go and let God, all would be okay. Imagine how I felt when I got that life-shattering call that you were gone.

I felt totally betrayed by my God. I felt like I had done something so horrible that he was punishing me by allowing my greatest fear to come true. I felt abandoned and alone. I questioned every belief I'd ever known. Feeling that I'd not only lost you, but also lost my trust in how the world should be.

It's taken years to rebuild my faith. To know that God did answer my prayers. He saved you, not my way but his. To this day God and I have an agreement. We agree to disagree on answered prayers.

Through my grief I have found many blessings. At first I felt abandoned, alone. Many friends walked away and never looked back. Apparently my grief made them uncomfortable, believing I should get over it and back to a so-called normal life. They wondered how they could be around someone who was so deeply grieving. Rather than helping me through, they simply disappeared. The years of friendship meant nothing. Shared experiences all forgotten. Grief scaring them so deeply, it was safer to abandon a friend than to stand by her side.

Isolation is a large part of how grief becomes complicated. I never believed what I'd heard but since living it, I know it's true. People forget you are still here. Forget you are trying to navigate through your new life, trying to survive without your child. Mourning the hopes and dreams once so alive now gone in the blink of an eye. No more phone calls or visits, just complete abandonment by people who were once considered close friends. You wake up one day and it hits. Not only have you lost a huge piece of your life, but you've also lost any connection to life outside your grief.

I also live that famous verse, "If God closes one door, He opens another." Through my grief I have found a new family. Other women who, like me, have suffered the ultimate loss. We share a bond and belong to a club we never wanted to join. Finding peace and strength through our loss. We lift each other on dark days. There is no need to defend our grief. No need to explain why those special days rebreak our healing hearts.

The gift of these friendships is priceless. Understanding that time does not heal all wounds. That healing has no deadline. That there is no shame in missing our children every day of our lives. We are a gift to one another.

Being honest with myself is tough. To realize that even after three years two months and twenty days, I'm still shocked by your death. To think that the years have passed without you here continues to take my breath away. Simple things still cause deep pain. A can of Beefaroni or hearing a song by Guns and Roses can be overwhelming. There are days when seeing a father with his baby reminds me of things that will never be.

I've learned that grief is not a race to be run. It's a process to be survived. A place to move through at our own pace. Grief is as individual as a fingerprint. My grief is mine alone. It is not something I should ever have to defend or be ashamed of.

Grief is love that has been rerouted. It lives in every fiber of our being. Grief is how we love.

Love never dies. It lasts forever. So does grief.

Imagining heaven

Matt,

Since your death I've been doing a lot of thinking about heaven. I want to know everything there is to know. I want to know if you're happy. If your heaven really is a beach. I have memories of us laughing sitting side by side watching the waves crash onto the shore and both saying, "Heaven is a beach." We were so alike. Our love of the sea is a tie that will forever bind us.

My bookshelves are lined with books written by those who had a near-death experience. I read their words, closing my eyes and letting my soul imagine the colors, shapes, and sounds. I see your smile in my mind. I hear the song of the gulls and remember the salty spray in my face. I see you as a child racing your brother through the waves. Your laughter was beautiful music to my ears. The vastness of the sea always made me feel the wonder of God.

I wonder about the nature of life after death. I search my Bible for comfort in knowing that you arrived in heaven and never looked back. Looking for answers anywhere they can be found, I scour bookstores like someone dying of thirst. I need to know.

There are days when the clouds roll into my heart and I question everything I believe. Those dark days bring such pain to my heart. Those are the days you'll find me talking out loud to God. Days I beg for a sign. My desperate heart needs proof. Those are the days I feel the weight of my grief, questioning everything I've ever believed about God and his heaven.

The hardest part of your death besides missing you every day is the wonder if I will ever see your handsome face again. So much was left unsaid and undone. Always thinking there would be more time. Never thinking you would leave me behind to find my new normal.

I wonder if you will be there when I leave this earth. You were never afraid to die. I remember our conversations, how you amazed me with your thoughts about God and heaven. How many times it was you comforting me. How ironic, a child giving peace to his mother.

I'm left with unanswerable questions that have power to haunt my broken heart. Questions that cause me to sit on the edge of the dark abyss of the unknown. Questions that shake me to my core. On those days I reach for my Bible. This amazing book spent so much time sitting on my shelf unopened. I talk to God, asking him to speak to me. To give me what I need to survive your loss and the emptiness that has taken up residence in my heart. Matt, I can hear you laughing as I write this. Your mom reads the Bible.

I found the following verse in John 14:

Let not your heart be troubled; you believe in God, believe also in me. In my father's house are many rooms, if it were not so I would have told you. I go to prepare a place for you. And if I go to prepare a place for you, I will come again and receive you to Myself; that where I am, you will be also.

Reading this verse filled my aching soul with a peace I haven't felt since you left.

I remember begging God to keep you safe. To take care of you until we were together again. Never did I think my prayers would be answered the way they were. Never did I think God would take you home before me. Your death broke my faith yet, at the same time, is helping to slowly rebuild it.

If you lived, my Bible probably would have remained unopened. Now the scriptures are where I run to on those rocky days. Sitting alone, my Bible opened looking for answers. I can feel you surround me with your peace. I close my eyes and see your face. Your beautiful eyes. Your smile. I see you walking near the most beautiful sea. The bluest water. Kahlua running by your side.

Oh, Matt, my beautiful boy, the sea continues to connect us. My dream is that one day when my eyes close on earth, they'll open again to see your beautiful eyes, face-to-face. Together we will run into the waves holding onto each other, never letting go. My grief will wash away with the tide. The gulls will sing a song of joy and Jesus will greet us saying, "Yes, my children, heaven is indeed a beach."

Matt's stone at a church memorial garden in Bear, Delaware.

Come, sit, grieve . . . repeat

Matt,

I could never have imagined the impact your death would have on every aspect of my life. Never did I ever think my grief would turn me into a leper. It seems people are terrified of those who are grieving. Scared to death of contact with me, or have that famous opinion on how long grief should last. I'm guessing my time is up. Even strangers run when I bring up addiction and your death. It's almost that I carry a contagious disease and if they get close enough, they'll carry it home to their family. Like the flu, only worse.

Unfortunately, your disease still carries an ugly stigma. I see the look on people's faces when they learn how you died. They can't get away fast enough. Quickly changing the subject as they scurry away. I feel like I have that huge *A* branded on my forehead. Except my *A* stands for addiction.

I still find it mindboggling that even today as we continue to lose people from all walks of life, addiction is still thought of as a dirty man's disease.

Experts on grief tell you to find a support group. Sounds easy, right? I had a better chance of being struck by lightning.

You see, Matt, my grief comes with a ton of baggage. All those what-ifs and I should-haves cling to my heart and take turns tearing little pieces away.

Death due to overdose comes with such regret. Things said and done dance with those things not said and not done. Until you have lived that rollercoaster with your child, one could ever understand the helplessness and hopelessness parents feel as we struggle to save our kids. Death from overdose is unlike any other loss. Not only do we struggle with grief, but the stigma continues to rear its ugly head, throwing daggers in our direction.

My attempts to find that group where I would fit in was futile. Believe me, I tried for several months. I sat next to mothers who lost their children to cancer and felt compassion ooze around the room. I remember sitting there feeling that familiar tightness grip my throat. Then it was death by car accident. Once again compassion.

I wanted to be Alice and slide down that rabbit hole. I wanted to be Jeannie, wiggling my nose and disappearing into thin air. I wanted to be anywhere but in that room when I said that ugly word, addiction, and felt their compassion wash away with the breaths of shock and stares.

Then it was off to another group who actually dealt with addiction. Oh, I had such high hopes. Finally, a group that got it. Imagine my surprise when I was subjected to another parent beaming with joy. My mind whirling as I realized this group was largely made up of parents whose kids were either in recovery or still active in addiction. My mind whirling, my gut revolting as I heard her voice praising God for saving her child. I felt like I'd been slapped. How dare God save her child and not mine! I remember wanting to run. Wanting once again to disappear. I made myself sit for an hour hearing more stories of recovery. Stories of continued struggles that I knew too well. I left sobbing and defeated.

I hid for months, licking my wounds, feeling isolated and alone. I scoured bookstores. My shelves now lined with books on grief and grieving. Reading the stories of other parents whose children also died from addiction gave me the push I needed.

I once read that when God closes one door, He opens another. As a nurse I've spend many years holding hands and shedding tears with people who lost a loved one. As a NICU nurse, I've also helped grieving parents say goodbye to their child. I remember praying, asking God what my purpose was now that you were gone. I spent the last seven years fighting to save you. Now I had all this time to discover my new path.

SADD, Support After Addiction Death, was born on a bitter rainy day. Sitting at my computer, I designed a pamphlet explaining how and why I was starting a support group exclusively for parents who lost a child to the misunderstood disease of addiction. Our pastor offered our church. The same church I said my final goodbye to you. The same church where your ashes were scattered in the garden I tend as we celebrated your first birthday in heaven.

Today I have a new family. Mothers and fathers who know and live the same grief that envelopes my life. We gather together and shed our tears. Our eyes mirror images of unfathomable pain. Lifting each other on those dark days when one of us is drowning. I look into their eyes and know no words are necessary. We have lived the nightmare.

Our ending is not the one we dreamed of, yet together we find strength in the blessing of finding each other. There is no shame, no stigma. Sharing pieces of our broken hearts we begin to slowly heal. Our children gone but never forgotten. Pictures are shared. Birthdays are remembered. Names are spoken. Many tears are shed. Memories are cherished.

God did close the door for me when it came to saving you. God also opened a new world where I can once more reach out, offer a hug and just show up. Grief doesn't scare this group. Grief is a part of who we are. Grief is the unwanted, unspeakable experience that bonds us more than blood.

As long as I live, I'll be grateful for the people who say your name, offer a hug, and stay.

Broken hearts don't show up on an ekg

Matt,

Since your death I've had several episodes where it feels like my heart is actually breaking apart. The medical community uses the term Broken Heart Syndrome. Although the cause isn't completely known, it's thought to be triggered by extreme emotional stress. Intense grief is listed as one of its causes. The heart is stunned by an unexpected, shocking event. When stunned, the heart no longer works efficiently and causes severe pain and anxiety.

I can tell you that I've become the posterchild for Broken Heart Syndrome. I've been in the emergency room more since your death than I have my entire life.

My first trip was the day before Christmas Eve. It was the first Christmas after your death and I think reality gut-punched me and began the shattering of my heart. I was a mess. Breathless and in

161

agony. Trying to describe my pain to doctors was like trying to explain color to a blind man. Nothing like your classic heart attack signs, just an unending ache deep in my soul.

I remember the doctor coming in to tell me all the tests were normal. Seriously, I thought. I'm dying and you're missing it. Then he asked what's been going on in my life. That simple question opened my floodgates. His face said it all. Your death, then my career screeching to a halt was tough enough, but when you threw in the death of a dear friend ten months later, I was drowning in grief.

Returning home, I felt so foolish. I was an active, healthy person. Why did I feel like I was dying? Once again I put one foot in front of the other, taking baby steps trying to navigate this new life.

Strike two was in April the following year. Year two was shaping up to be another brutal round of reality. I made it through all those firsts and never expected the seconds to come with stronger gut-punches. I was in my garden clearing out old leaves and trying to remember the joy I once felt digging in the dirt. My garden was my sanctuary, the place I fled to find peace during your addiction.

Seeing your cigarette butts was a sharp slap across my face. Memories flooded my brain. You sitting on the deck pitching your smoked butts into my precious gardens. I remember yelling at your disrespect for all my hard work. What should have been a minor fix turned into a major fight as you continued to flick your butts into the garden with that look of defiance on your face. Oh God, that memory long since buried was now dancing through my head. I held them to my nose trying to pick up the scent of your mouth. Oh God, what I would give to have you sitting there again. This time I would hold you and hug you knowing how our journey would end.

Once again that familiar pain shot across my chest. Struggling to catch my breath. That lump in my throat growing larger each second. This time I'm sure something will show up. My heart was hurting so badly, yet once again everything was normal. Sent home once again feeling foolish. Even my nursing education wasn't any help in controling the thought that I must be dying.

Strike three arrived five days after returning home from Florida. Even the beauty of the Keys couldn't lift my grief. I felt it the second week there. I could see you everywhere and nowhere. Dear God, you died in Florida, was all I could think. You should've been enjoying the turquoise water. We should be having lunch. I should be seeing your place, meeting your friends.

You should be alive.

Returning home was another slap of reality. My eyes finding your urn. Seeing your smiling face staring back at me forever frozen in time. I can't breathe. This time I heard my heart break. Feeling the shards of glass tearing into my throat. I can't be alive and survive this pain. I must be dying.

Once again the doctor wants to know what's been happening in my life. Once again I see the look of compassion for your broken mother on her face.

This time a stress test is ordered. I'm injected with an isotope and told to start walking. The treadmill belt is moving. I think of you. I'm walking too fast. Trying to run from reality. I'm told to slow down. The speed needs to build up. All I want to do is run. Pictures are taken and reviewed by the heart experts. I'm told I have a beautiful, healthy heart. I sit and listen as tears run down my face. How can they not see the cracks, the shards that live where my heart used to?

The nurse practitioner gives me a hug. Tears mingling with mine. She, too, knows living with a broken heart, losing her daughter years ago. She tells me a mother's heart never forget. Eventually the breaks won't be as severe and gut-wrenching. Time will eventually put some pieces back where they belong. One day my heart will remember only the love rather than the loss.

Until then I've learned that a heart breaking never makes noise. It's only felt by the soul of the one experiencing the pain, unseen to the human eye but deeply felt by the griever. And like grief, the break signifies unspeakable, unending love.

To my son on Mother's Day

Matt,

This Sunday is Mother's Day. My fourth without you. I actually had to stop and count the years. I was so shocked and breathless that I needed to count the years on my fingers like a preschooler. May of 2015, 2016, 2017, and now 2018.

Four years and I'm still having trouble believing you won't be calling or walking through my door.

Today is only Friday yet I feel that familiar grief grabbing for and tightening its grip on my heart. I've tried hard to not go there, to forget that this Sunday is *that* day that honors all mothers. Unfortunately, every other commercial shows kids and flowers. Smiling mothers giving hugs and kisses to their precious children.

I've kept very busy today. Cleaning out closets, exchanging winter clothes for summer. Cleaning like the energizer bunny. Trying to keep my brain occupied and away from what is coming. As fate would have it, or maybe it was you, a box of pictures fell from a shelf to my closet floor. I found your smiling face staring back at me. I could no longer fight. Seeing your picture, knowing there would be no more, shattered the pieces of my already broken heart. I slid to the floor and cried like a wounded animal. Raw, guttural sounds flying from my battered soul.

I tried to resist looking further but my hands were already searching through the scattered prints searching for more of you. Pictures from years ago. You and Mike standing side by side. Two precious smiling faces. Brothers, one year and twenty days apart. People called you Irish twins. I called you double trouble. I never remember seeing one without the other.

Memories of past Mother's Days flooded my mind. My two boys running into the house, hands full of buttercups and dandelions.

"Happy Mother's Day," your little voices shouted together.

When you got older, my gifts became more sophisticated. Pieces of jewelry or a hand-painted picture.

After Mike left for the Coast Guard, you realized how much he was missed. You never failed to remember my day. A card, flowers, or a surprise visit. Distance never mattered. You'd leave your precious beach and spend the day with me. You were never too old for a hug or to say, "I love you, Mom."

Now, I'm left with precious memories. Cards from Mother's Days long ago. Oh God, how precious they have become. Treasured pieces of paper signed by you. I've kept them all these years, never thinking they would become so priceless. I run my finger along your signature remembering teaching you to write. Never thinking that one day your unique signature would be something left behind that would bring both joy and unspeakable pain to your mother's heart. Both my boys so precious. One now gone forever.

Mother's Day, once a day I looked so forward to, has become a day of loss. Memories of two boys becoming men. Always showing up together to surprise their mom. Both so handsome, sharing childhood antics that bonded them forever. Stories kept secret from Mom, being shared with howls of laughter. Mother's Day is now so different from anything I could ever have imagined.

This year I will give myself a gift. I will allow myself the luxury of tears. Tears I hide from the world will flow as I remember you as a young man bounding through my door with flowers in your hand. Your handsome face. Your smile filling my heart with joy. I will allow memories to fill my mind. I will reaffirm that I will always be your mother and you will always be my son. Our connection continuing through time and space.

I will pray for a sign, a feeling from you, your gift to me on this most painful day. Be the rays of the sun gently kissing my face. Be the tender breeze whispering in my ear. Be that puffy cloud or the cardinal in my garden. Be with me in spirit as I remember your love as both a child and as a man.

My love for you will live on forever. A bond stronger than death. A mother's love transcending time and space. Her youngest son gone, forever holding a piece of her heart.

In Memory Of

Matt
7/30/77-1/3/15

Heaven's a little closer in a house by the sea

Matt,

It's Memorial Day weekend. The weather is cloudy and gray. You have been gone three years and four months. I still find myself shocked when reality hits.

I remember when you lived at the beach. You hated summers. All the traffic and crowds. I can still hear your voice complaining about how long it took to get from one place to another. What I wouldn't give to have you here complaining about summer tourists invading your paradise. I can still see you standing in your boat. "The only way to get anywhere around here is by boat."

You had that large grin on your handsome face. I knew this was just an excuse to get out on the water, your favorite place to be.

I dreamed about your house the other night. I drove by and saw it was for sale. I sat in my car calling the realtor. I had to get inside. I had to be where you were. She was kind and listened as I told her this house once belonged to you. I told her I desperately needed to walk through those rooms once again. I had to touch where you touched.

She told me she had adult sons and couldn't imagine what I was feeling. Handing me the keys without any questions. My tears started to fall as the lock turned and the door opened. My mind flooded with memories of walking through this door hundreds of times before.

The house was vacant. Eerily quiet. Looking exactly as it was the last time we walked through these rooms together. Both of us with tears in our eyes, knowing your disease robbed us of our happy place.

I sat on the living room floor, the carpet showing signs of wear. Familiar spills and puppy accidents marking years of our life were still apparent. Each mark told a story. I could picture our house the way it used to be. Full of love and laughter. Sandy dogs running through the kitchen after romping in the surf. Both of us trying to shoo them outside, laughing as we became as sandy as the dogs.

I remembered every detail. Every moment we shared together. Ten years of wonderful memories flooded my brain. My mind allowed me the gift of going back in time. I could see you standing in the kitchen. Khaki shorts, bare feet, sun-kissed hair.

"Hey, Mom, can I get you a drink?"

Your face handsome and tan. Your beautiful eyes always smiling. You loved this house by the sea. I loved your happiness.

I walked from room to room as precious memories washed over my shattered heart. Memories of a time when life was perfect.

Settlement day. Moving in. Hanging pictures. Sandy floors. The chaos of boxes everywhere. The joy that living by the sea brought to both of us. Oh, how proud you were of the life you built. I remember that beautiful smile.

"Mom, can you believe this is mine?"

How I wished I had the power to go back in time. I wanted to open my eyes and see you standing there, wanted to undo the ugliness that took you away. I wanted to wake up from the nightmare that is now reality.

I felt a profound sadness wash over me. Still in disbelief that you were gone. Oh God, how did this happen? How did life take this ugly turn? I felt your loss like never before.

This once cozy little home so full of life, love, and laughter now stood as empty as my soul. Tears began again as I walked through that door for the last time. This house now a symbol of profound loss.

Walking to my car, I allowed myself one last look. My mind is playing tricks on my heart as I see you coming through the door. That smile on your face. Your sun-bleached hair hidden under your hat, Kahlua bouncing at your heels. For a brief moment you were there. I wanted to yell out. To reach toward you and touch your face. For a fleeting second everything returned to normal.

Life was as it used to be. I felt joy.

I remember hearing the saying, "Heaven is a little closer in a house by the sea."

Imagine my surprise finding that print while visiting a seaside town. I couldn't wait to hang it in our little house that represented heaven to both of us. I remember standing on a chair trying to guide you. A little to the right. No just a smidge left. Perfect.

That print became the wall centerpiece, surrounded by pictures we both loved. The dogs running through the breaking waves. You standing by your precious boat. You and Mike swimming in the bay. Both of you tanned and smiling. Pictures of a life that now feels a lifetime ago. Almost like a dream.

Those memories live forever protected and preserved in my heart. That loved print now hangs in my home. Seeing it tugs at my heart. Its meaning now signifies unspeakable loss. The casualties of addiction.

My beautiful boy and a little piece of heaven by our beloved sea.

Can of Beefaroni and so much more

Matt,

Never in a million years did I think I would ever fall apart in the pasta aisle of the grocery store after seeing a can of Beefaroni. The gut-wrenching, hit-my-heart-hard kind of pain left me holding onto my cart, telling myself to breathe. Tears running down my face like a hose stuck in the on position with no hope of being turned off.

Oh God, I think, how am I ever going to survive the rest of my life if can't even make it through the grocery store without a major meltdown? Seeing that can of Beefaroni and feeling those feelings has become part of my new life I never saw coming or signed up for.

Beefaroni was your favorite food. I would stock up at the ten-for-ten-dollars sale and hurry home to stuff your weekly care package with all your favorite foods. Sending them off with a piece of my heart to the halfway house you lived in a thousand miles away from home.

A can of Beefaroni, a connection to my son who is no more.

Then there is the scent of Phoenix. This was your smell. I can still hear your voice, "Hey, Mom, can you pick me up my deodorant? I'm running low."

I've found myself in this same store walking to the deodorant aisle and finding that familiar blue can. I remove the lid and spray a tiny bit. Closing my eyes and taking a deep breath, I let my mind drift back to happier times. This is what my life has become, finding pieces of you in everyday places, trying to keep our connection alive.

I once felt that being the mother of a son suffering from addiction was the worst thing that ever happened to my life. That constant feeling of helplessness and anxiety ruled my mind. I compared your addiction to being trapped on a very fast, very high rollercoaster with many twists and turns. Never knowing what each day would bring, what was coming, or how some days would end.

Mothers of addicts learn to live with the crazy unpredictability that goes hand-in-hand with the disease. We learn to expect the unexpected and relish the thought that recovery is possible. Your addiction became mine as I held onto the rollercoaster for dear life. Praying for things to somehow calm down and allow us both a little piece of normal. I've since learned that being the mother of an addict who suffered an accidental overdose is waking up and finding the nightmare you feared most has now become your reality.

Be careful what you pray for, they say. I prayed for peace, I prayed for quiet, I prayed for your addiction to go away. My prayers have been answered but not in the way I imagined. I now struggle to survive in this all too quiet, empty new world. I long for the days of chaos. Riding the uncertainty on the rollercoaster known as addiction now feels like a walk in the park compared to being the one left behind.

Learning to navigate through my grief is a daily process. I'm now the lone rider on a different coaster. This one mimics the other but now the ups and downs belong solely to me. There are days I wake up, shed my tears, pray for strength and somehow get through. There are days when the darkness overrides my heart and I crawl through my brokenness as if it is surrounded by shards of glass, each piercing my heart with knifelike accuracy.

For now, I take it one day at a time. I pray that someday a can of Beefaroni or the scent of Phoenix will warm my heart, not break it. Reminding me of the connection between a mother and her son that neither time nor space can break. For now, I pray for understanding and strength as I continue to put one foot in front of the other while attempting to navigate an unchartered life without my son.

I know I will never return to the person I once was. Going back to that person is not an option. She vanished when you died. Gone with your last breath.

My grief path is my own. It's rocky and full of broken pieces from a life that used to be. I tread lightly on days I can. I crawl through the glass on days when the pain kills, and I question my survival.

My grief has no finish line. It's one day, one breath, one scream at a time.

My grief is the best I can do. Navigating this path is the most painful thing I've ever had to do.

One thing I know for sure is I'm not okay. I will never be okay. And for me that just has to be okay.

Life will never be the same

Matt,

Today would have been your forty-first birthday. I should be on my way to the beach to spend time with you on your special day. We would have headed for the beach, walked the dogs, letting them run through the surf while we caught up on life. We would have planned our dinner feast of crabs, shrimp, and beer.

But today our reality is much different from my dreams for this day. For you are forever thirty-seven and this is your fourth birthday in heaven.

Today I spent the morning letting my grief pour out from my soul, looking through every album I own with pictures of our life. Beautiful memories flooded my broken heart as I asked myself how this nightmare became our reality. Pictures of you with that smile and those beautiful eyes staring back at me through all the phases of your life. From infancy through adulthood. Looking so happy and healthy. It is so hard for me to understand this reality. My brain knows you are gone. My heart struggles with this truth.

Today there will be no family party. No cake, no funny card. I will never see you with your brother standing side by side laughing about how you're both over the big four-oh.

Comparing how childhood dreams became a reality or remained still a dream.

Losing you is losing a future of love, laughter, and memories. Losing you is never seeing my sons together again. Never hearing your laughter as you tell of childhood antics that were kept secret from mom. Losing you is never meeting the girl who stole your heart. Losing you is never dancing at your wedding. Losing you is never sharing your joy of holding your newborn child for the first time. Losing you has taken its toll on me.

Losing you is losing me

Reality is that I will never see you coming through my door with your children in tow. That smile and those eyes forever gone. No mini Matts for me to spoil and hug. No babes to be rocked to sleep. No babes to soothe my aching heart. No future generation to share stories of your childhood antics. No more of you.

Your brother will never know the joy of being an uncle. He will never take your son fishing or show your daughter treasures saved from your childhood. He will never know the joy of holding his brother's children in his arms or teaching them to run through the surf with you by his side. He will never watch his younger brother discover the joys and heartbreaks of being a parent. He will never be able to offer advice or share his list of dos and don'ts of fatherhood. There will be no more children squealing with joy as that new puppy comes running into their arms. No more brothers sharing the secret of what makes a house a home.

How I wish heaven had visiting hours. I would throw myself into your arms and never let you go. I would tell you how much your loss has changed my life. I would tell you over and over again how much I love you. I would beg you to stay with me forever.

Today I will honor your life. I will let my grief have its way. Today I will let my tears flow, no longer fighting or pretending that I am okay. Today I will remember the joy you brought to my life. I will allow myself to feel the profound loss of your death. Today I will close my eyes and remember your hugs, your voice, your smile.

Today I will wrap myself up in you.

Matt holding a rescue kitten visiting with his brother Mike and his dog Sparky in Florida, while Mike served in the U.S. Coast Guard.

Wrapping us up with you

Matt,

I had myself fooled. Thinking that after forty-three months, I'd be able to walk into your closet and not lose what was left of my mind.

A friend offered to make a quilt from your shirts, and I so wanted this to happen. I remember giving myself a peptalk all morning, telling myself to be strong. I kept saying to myself over and over again, "You can do this."

I kept telling myself it was time to go through your clothing and donate some to a homeless shelter, knowing you would approve. I kept telling myself that your sweaters and coats would help keep a stranger warm this winter.

I kept thinking how wasteful it was to keep everything just as it was when you were alive. Like you would come walking through the door looking for your favorite sweater. Like I was expecting you to come up to the kitchen freshly showered, smelling of Phoenix, telling me about your workday.

Your closet was the biggest in the house. A huge walk-in fully carpeted and lined with shelves. Before you moved home, I used it for storing winter coats and odds and ends that I couldn't decide what to do with. I remember putting my hand on the door, giving myself that last push. Once again telling myself I could do this.

Pushing through the doors allowed light to flood the room. I stood surrounded by you. Your t-shirts and sweaters neatly folded on the shelves, jackets hanging in the order last worn.

I closed my eyes and took a deep breath as I sat on the floor and started to unfold your clothing. I didn't realize the power of my grief. I started to bury my face in your clothing. Pulling things off hangers and wrapping myself up in sweaters, coats, and anything I could get my hands on. I didn't understand the sounds coming from the depths of my soul had broken through the silence of the house.

I hadn't realized that I was no longer alone sobbing on your closet floor until I felt her wet nose. Belle lay down next to me, trying to comfort me with her body. Like me, she buried her nose in your clothing, occasionally lifting her head and smelling the air. I could see it in her eyes that her heart recognized your smell just like mine did.

Belle tilted her head when I mentioned your name. Like me, she was looking for you.

We sat together for most of the afternoon. Belle laying in the pile, me wrapped up in the mess I'd created. Both of us smelling each piece trying to recover your scent. Every shirt held a bittersweet memory. Each one telling a story. Some came from travels to the Caribbean. Some you bought just because you couldn't stop laughing after reading their message. In my mind I could picture you wearing each one. Some were captured in the photos lining our bookshelves.

I lost track of time as I allowed myself the gift of grieving you with no one to witness my brokenness. Just the dog we both loved. I sat talking to Belle as if she understood. I talked about you and I walking together on the beach as Belle and Kahlua played in the surf. I talked about all the times we shared with the dogs in our happy place. I told her how she lived with you while I found a new home. I told her you constantly told me she was your dog now, and you weren't giving her back with that big grin on your face.

I swear she understood as her snout continued to smell the air surrounding us. I let myself relax into her as memories of happy times at the beach flooded my brain. It was as if my dam broke, and all the tears and memories were released together.

I don't remember putting your things in a bin. I think that fog settled into my brain. The fog that protected my psyche as I drove to my dear friend's home and allow her to transform the most precious pieces left of your life.

I remember sobbing as I placed the bin in her arms, almost as if I was a new mom turning over my precious child to the care of another. She asked if I wanted to assist her in how the quilt would be put together, wanting me to give her guidance in how to create a piece to honor your life.

I just couldn't do it. As ashamed as I was of my inability to help, I was emotionally spent. I would never survive holding those precious pieces so soon before I could begin to repair my shattered soul.

She called days later, your quilt was complete.

Emotions swam through my brain. I wasn't ready to face the reality of what your quilt would represent. These shirts would never be worn by you again. This reality hit over and over as I drove through blinding tears to pick you up bringing you home again.

Walking through her door, I saw the masterpiece. The quilt was displayed on her couch. I put my hand over my mouth to cover my sobs as she wrapped me in her hug. She laid the quilt in my arms like a precious newborn. I drink you in, holding you and burying my face into you. Heading home, I placed you on the passenger seat and talked to you as I did when you were alive.

Arriving home, I carried you upstairs and laid you across my bed. Belle now by my side, her nose seeking your scent. We sat next to each other, a grieving mother and her loyal dog sharing a loss felt deeply by both. Wrapped up together with the memories of the boy we both loved and lost.

OCTOBER 21, 2018

As the seasons continue to change, my grief remains unchanged

Matt,

It's hard for me to believe that you have been gone for forty-five months and eighteen days. But who's counting? Right. I am. I've been counting the days as they turned from weeks to months, then from months to years.

I've watched as spring brings new life to the earth. Plants burst forth in a riot of color. Birds fly in and out of the garden houses, building nests in anticipation of new life. The summer sun warms my soul as the earth continues its beautiful transformation. In the blink of an eye summer becomes fall. Magnificent colors continue to mark the earth with incredible beauty. Before long a cold wind blows, bringing in the darkness that announces the arrival of winter.

The changing seasons remind me of another time of counting. I counted the months while carrying you. Praying we would make it past that first trimester, sailing along until you decided to announce yourself to my world. You were a summer baby.

You became an incredible man who died on a cold winter day. You took your first breath on July 30, and your last on January 3.

I look at your stone and compare the Js and threes, asking myself the question that has no answer. Why?

I started a garden to honor you. To have a place to come and talk to you, a place to scream and cry. To be alone in the grief that continues to grip my heart when I see your name engraved on that stone. You never wanted to be in the ground. Some of your ashes are here, scattered. Your garden changes with the seasons yet my grief remains the same.

Some days it hits without warning. I will be digging in the cool soil, clearing out the old plants while planning for the new. My mind focusing on colors and smells. A memory hits of another time when we knelt side by side planting flowers in another garden. Both muddy and laughing as the dogs did their best to trample our new plantings. I can hear your laughter and see your smile. I am reduced to tears as that one poignant memory leads to another.

As the seasons change, your garden follows. Summer perennials attract butterflies and colorful birds. Summer brings another reminder that you will be forever thirty-seven. Summer brings birthday candles to your garden. I light them and sing out loud. Watching the flames flicker in the soft breeze. I wait for them to blow out and wonder if you are there with me.

Memories of past celebrations come and join us. Days when we thought time was on our side. That birthdays would never end as abruptly as they did. The peace of the garden hugs my heart, allowing my grief to be present.

Fall brings new beauty to your garden. Mums in an array of blazing colors surround your stone. Dead flowers are removed, allowing room for a new brightness. Bright red cardinals surround the feeder as falling leaves cover the damp grass. An unwanted reminder that soon the ground will freeze and the season of planting will be done.

Winter brings a deep stillness to your garden. It will surrender to sleep just as you did that cold January morning. Do not fear. My need to feel close leads me back to you. I will continue to come and brush the snow off your stone. I will continue to tend to your garden as I tend to my heart. I will keep the feeder full, giving the cardinals a reason to come. I will sit quietly, allowing my grief a place to be as the seasons change and memories find me.

Similar to the passage of time and the changing of the seasons my grief marches on.

Matt with our rescue pup, Scarlett. One of my last pictures of Matt.

Searching for a new normal

Matt,

The definition of normal is something that conforms to a general pattern, ordinary or usual, typical, something that would be expected. I can tell you that I've been searching for normal for forty-six months.

Ever since you died, nothing has felt normal. It's not normal for a mother to bury her child. There is nothing normal about having to visit your child at a memorial garden. Nothing ordinary about not being able to pick up the phone and hear your voice. Nothing expected as I put my hands on your urn in my attempt to feel close to you.

It's not normal to feel like you're choking every day. Not normal to feel like your heart split in half but still remains beating in your chest. My emotions are wild, changing from moment to moment.

Memories still have the power to bring me to my knees. Normal is not breaking down when hearing a song, seeing a young father holding hands with his child, or having to choke back tears as two little brothers ring your doorbell yelling, "Trick or treat."

It's not normal to walk around on unstable ground, feeling foggy and anxious. I've suffered through losses before. This is worlds apart from anything I have ever lived through. This normal was never expected. What *was* expected was you to grow old. To marry. To be in my life until it was time for me to go, not you. Normal is burying your parents, not your child.

So how do I find my new normal? I've heard that term so much I want to scream. How in the hell can anything be normal after your child has died? I know people mean well. People who have never lost a child are so quick to tell me how to adjust to this new phase in my life. Really? people who can hug their kids, call their kids, share meals with their kids telling me that this is my new normal?

These well-meaning strangers have never ridden my emotional rollercoaster. They don't experience my triggers. They haven't been hit by the grief bus that returns time and time again to slam me over and over. They don't get the fact that my future has changed. Plans, goals, and dreams are no more. My brain gets it yet my heart struggles to accept the collateral damage that I walk through every day.

Believe me, I have trouble believing that after all the time that has passed, I'm still breathless when reality hits. That forty-six months feels like yesterday. That there is no way that we are two months away from the four-year mark. My brain screams how, how, how have I survived this long? How can it truly be that I have not heard your voice or seen your smile for almost four years?

There is nothing normal about not having your child in your life. There is nothing normal about having to put on your mask to face a world that is terrified of the grieving. I've learned that this so-called new normal is just a polite way to tell grieving parents to get over it. It's just one of those new terms that's supposed to fix our broken lives.

What I've learned is that life will never be normal. Whether it be new or not, there is nothing normal about losing a child. I've also come to understand that grief has no timetable, it follows no predictable course. Nothing about grief is normal. It is a personal journey that no one can walk for you.

Grief is heartbreaking, complicated, powerful, and unbalancing. It is anything but normal.

Matt with a friend on the beach in Boca Raton, 2014.

The space you left behind

Matt,

Today is Thanksgiving. I can feel the grief stalking me. I try to keep my mask in place as I face this bittersweet day, that battered mask I wear hiding my true heartbreak from the world.

Today is a day to give thanks for all the blessings we have received throughout the year. Yes, I know I have been blessed. I have my health, my home, a loving husband. I have your brother and a beautiful grand-daughter. I don't mean to sound ungrateful, but your loss puts my life into a different perspective. What I long for is to have you here.

Memories of past Thanksgivings flood my brain. I close my eyes and go back to a time when holidays were full of crazy family chaos. I can see you and Mike standing side by side frying the turkey. Laughter surrounds your faces like frozen breaths of air. I can still hear your voices and see your heads almost touching as you tried to keep your conversation from drifting into the house. The rest of us inside staying warm, sipping wine as we prepared the rest of our feast. The dogs underfoot trying to grab whatever morsel of food that fell to the floor. My heart was full of gratitude having both my boys and my family under one roof to celebrate our blessings and each other.

Thanksgiving 2014 would be your last Thanksgiving on earth. If only I had known. You were in a sober home in Florida, when your addiction reared its ugly, unrelenting head once again. I was celebrating with family at home, but my heart was in Florida with you. Your absence left a void that nothing could fill. As we sat around the table, I dialed your number, longing to make you part of the family's conversation. Your voice sounded amazing. Clear and strong. I pictured your smile as you shared your holiday plans with us. You were gathering with friends to share turkey and fellowship. You sounded excited about life once again. I could hear the old Matt back in your voice. Although I missed you terribly, I knew your recovery was priority over my wanting you home.

As I passed the phone around the table, everyone agreed how great you sounded. We were all so proud of your recovery and looked forward to future holidays together. If only I had known.

I stalked your Facebook page alone in the dark that night. Family gone. The house cleaned and quiet. I needed to see your face and convince myself I could relax and trust that my blessings would continue with your recovery. You posted the best picture of you with friends. Happy smiling faces wrapped up in one big hug. I have that picture in a frame. I stare at your face in disbelief. If only I had known.

There's nothing silent about the night

Matt,

Tis the season. Christmas music plays wherever I go. I can't even run into the grocery store without being punched in the gut. There is no escaping the joy of the season. People with smiles on their glowing faces are singing along to the carols.

The song "I'll Be Home For Christmas," left me sobbing in the cereal aisle. I want to scream, "No! He won't be home this Christmas, or next!"

I wanted to stand in the middle of that aisle and scream at the top of my lungs, "My son is dead. Everyone shut up!"

There is no merry or happy in my holiday.

Sleep used to be my reprieve. The only time when I could crawl under the covers and disappear. The quiet of the night used to bring a comfort to my soul like nothing else. Wrapping myself up in my safe cocoon, I could shut out the happy noises of the world and just be.

I don't know what the trigger was. I don't understand why, but suddenly the night became my enemy. The silence I once craved is now full of noise. Like a newborn babe, my brain has confused day and night. Maybe it's the season. Maybe it's ugly reality. Perhaps my grief found my safe place and decided to move in. Quietly, with the cunning of a predator, grief found me in the silence of the night.

Now, like a child fearing the monster in the closet, I dread the night. The night awakens all those thoughts that were safely buried in my psyche. Those visions of your disease swirling through my head. The what-ifs and whys flood my brain, ripping me from the safety of slumber. My body instantly reacts, causing my heart to pound and hot tears to form. There will be no escape from the questions that continue to tug at my heart.

The silence. The lack of distractions allows my eyes to focus on your picture smiling back at me in the night. My mind goes to places I refuse to visit in the daylight. The darkness, the stillness, has a way of surrounding me with the despair I can no longer outrun. The darkness allows the grief a power that is nonexistent in daylight.

In my mind I have conversations with you. I pray for your peace, and mine. I wipe my tears as my mind dances between acceptance and disbelief. I allow myself memories of how holidays used to be, when I was the one singing in the aisles with a smile on my face and childlike anticipation for our gathering in my heart.

I've come to realize that nothing will ever be the same. Holidays will never get easier. I will continue to feel your loss as long as I walk the earth. Certain Christmas carols will most certainly come with gut-punches.

Sleepless nights have become part of my present life, reminding me of past sleepless nights when I held you close and rocked you as a baby. Holding your sweet body next to mine those nights, bonding us forever. Under the cover of darkness I will close my eyes and try to remember your smell. Your laugh. Your amazing eyes. I will allow the darkness to hide my weeping from the world. I will allow myself to imagine you spending the holidays in a beautiful peace. I will lay in the darkness and allow myself to grieve.

Matt at home for Christmas with pups Kahlua and Beau.

DECEMBER 25, 2018

All I want for Christmas is a redo

Matt,

It's Christmas day. My fourth Christmas without you. I heard the song "All I Want For Christmas Is You," and thought what I really want is a redo. I want to redo our entire lives. I want Father Time to give me the power to turn back the clock to when you and Mike were young boys. I want to take back this knowledge of how our lives would unravel and redirect our outcome.

I want to go back to the Christmases of complete chaos. The ones when a flu bug hit all of us and we took turns running to the bathroom while struggling to open presents from Santa. I want to return to that time in life when Christmas brought great joy to my heart. Watching both my boys laughing as wrapping paper piled up under the tree.

I want to go back to your teenage years. Knowing now that your career choice would lead to your ultimate death, I'd give up everything to have known that one day your passion for cars would lead to injury that would then turn into a deadly disease.

If only I had the knowledge then that I have now, perhaps you would be sharing Christmas with me.

I want to go back to your surgery and rip that prescription from your hands. I want to make the nightmare of your addiction magically disappear. I want the ghost of Christmas past to come and sweep me away from the reality of Christmas present.

I want to hear the doorbell ring and see you walk in with a wife and kids in tow. I want to once again watch you and Mike sitting side by side as you tear into festive wrapping paper, laughing over the gifts from your crazy mom. I want to hear your voices, your laughter. I want pictures showing both my boys together as men.

I want to never take anything for granted. I would treat every Christmas as if it could be our last together. Enjoying every moment of chaos. Every moment of laughter. I would have hugged you longer. I would have taken more pictures of us together. I would have spent more time memorizing your face.

I remember watching *A Charlie Brown Christmas* with you and Mike. Never thinking that one day those words so innocently spoken by Charlie Brown would shatter what's left of my broken heart.

Material things, gifts, and decorations mean nothing when those you love are missing from around the Christmas tree.

Nothing happy about my new year

Matt,

Today is December 31, the final day of 2018. I'm fighting my demons. Trying to stay away from that dark place where I sit on that slippery slope. The place where memories become almost too painful that I fight to keep them out of my head.

Our last New Year's Eve was December 31, 2014. We were one thousand miles apart. I was sitting watching the snowfall and the ball drop to welcome 2015 into our lives. You were sitting on a beach attending an outdoor Narcotics Anonymous meeting. Two different places but with hearts connected.

We spoke briefly. I told you how proud I was of you and your newfound sobriety. We talked about how your life was finally getting back on track. We talked about our expectations for 2015, and started the countdown until we would see each other again. I was so looking forward to getting out of this cold and joining you on a sunny beach.

We ended our call with I love yous, as we always did. I saw your Facebook post about doing the right thing. You were posting about attending a meeting on New Year's Eve instead of partying. My heart was so happy to read those words.

My hope for 2015 was to have you back. That my amazing Matt was coming back to the surface, the Matt I knew before the demons took over your soul.

Gazing at the stars on that crisp night, I sent a prayer to heaven to keep you safe. I fell asleep thinking we had survived your addiction and this new year would bring us both peace.

Two days later, you were dead. It was January 3, 2015.

That day, hopes and dreams for a happy new year shattered at my feet. That day my soul shattered like a glass thrown against a concrete wall into too many pieces to salvage.

So here I am facing another New Year's Eve with only memories to soothe my broken heart. Facing the fact that January 3 is coming again. Reality is difficult to comprehend, the fact that 2018 will be gone in the blink of an eye, at the drop of a ball, as smiling people begin their resolutions for this new year.

My heart is jealous of the happy crowds. Those people who have no idea how painful it is to watch 2014 or 2018 disappear to the count of ten. Ushering in a new year is not what I want to do. I want that ball to go backwards. I want that ball not to drop but to travel back in time. I want the new year to be an old year returning to when you were alive.

A month after you died, I received a box from Florida. It contained a few of your personal possessions. As I opened the box, your smell surrounded my being. The hat you wore to your meeting on New Year's Eve was staring back at me. Immediately that photo of you flashed through my brain. I could see your smiling face as you blew a horn welcoming in 2015.

I can't tell you how many times through the years I've run my hands over your hat. I cover my face searching for your scent. I hold that hat close to my heart as if I'm giving you a New Year's hug.

Tonight I will let my tears flow at will. Tonight I will gaze at the stars and send a prayer that you are at peace spending this night celebrating in heaven. Tonight I allow myself to feel what I feel, taking each moment as I can.

Tonight, watching the ball drop will be a painful reminder that time does not stop marching on.

YEAR 4

Letters to Matt

I never expected this

Matt,

Today is January 3. The fourth anniversary of your death. The weather mimics my spirit, cold and gloomy. I've made no plans for today. I just can't come to the beach and walk where we once did. I've chosen to just be and let my grief have its way.

I can remember every moment after hearing those words I prayed never to hear four years ago. At 12:15 p.m., while taking care of ill babies, I learned that you were gone.

I remember a feeling of leaving my body to escape the pain of my heart breaking. I remember someone screaming, never thinking it was me . . .

I remember hearing words telling me to breathe, to sit, to drink. I remember how badly I wanted my heart to stop beating so I could be where you were.

Four years later, I still seek you, expecting you to come through my door with Kahlua at your heels. I expect you to grab a drink from the fridge and suck it down from the carton, laughing at me as I try to force a glass into your hand.

I expect you at the dinner table as we share stories about our day. I expect you to give me a hug and to hear, "Love you, Mom," before you descend the stairs to your mancave. I never expected this. This overwhelming, never-ending, life-shattering grief. I never expected to lose you so suddenly and unexpectedly. I never thought that pictures and memories would be all that was left of our life.

I never expected that four years later my heart would still be screaming as it was the moment you left me behind. I never expected that I would constantly be looking for signs, searching the clouds for angels and crosses, for stones and leaves in the shape of hearts.

I never expected to have my breath sucked out of my lungs after seeing a can of Beefaroni in the grocery isle. I never expected to have a meltdown at the moment I hear a song or see the waves hitting the shore where we once walked together.

I never expected that seeing two little boys playing together would cause a physical ache in my soul. I never expected that seeing two fathers laughing together while watching their children play would remind me of what I would never see now that you are gone.

I never expected to be this person, a ghost of who I used to be. The eyes staring back at me break my heart. I never expected to be the one left behind.

I never expected the pain of losing you would continue to be so powerful and soul crushing. I never expected that four years later the tears would still fall as they did in the early days. I never expected to visit a garden bearing a stone engraved with your name.

I never expected to fight for my sanity. I never expected to walk this painful journey. I never expected that life would turn out as it has. I never expected to live this painful lesson of not taking a day for granted. I never expected to be writing letters to you that you would never read. I never expected any of what I live with since your death. I never expected you to die.

Four years later. I never expected this.

Surviving those aftershocks

Matt,

An aftershock is defined as a small earthquake that follows a large earthquake. It generally occurs in the same area where the main shock occurred and is caused by the displacement of the earth following that first main shock.

Part of living through earthquakes is learning to live with aftershocks. It's obvious I lived through my first major quake.

January 3, 2015, my world was hit with a quake of unmeasurable magnitude. That day, my life was knocked off its axis and left free-spinning into an atmosphere of shock and immeasurable grief.

Since that day, these unexpected aftershocks hit just when my mind starts to feel stable once again. I've read aftershocks can last for years. I'm living proof of that truth. Four years and ten days have passed, and the ground beneath my feet remains unsteady.

Grief is a lot like aftershocks. One never knows when the shaking, unstable feeling will strike. Usually there is no warning. A thought, a memory, a word can bring on the most unsteady of feelings. Almost like the ground is moving under my feet, it's a feeling of being out of control, wondering what is happening, and why now.

I've come to understand that most of what has been written about grief is untrue. Grief knows no time limit. It doesn't lessen as the years pass. It doesn't let go after you have passed all those firsts.

Grief certainly doesn't follow any stages or steps. It knows no boundaries. There are no certain series of programs or steps to follow to get you through to the end. Because there really is no end. Grief is the journey of aftershocks that hit unexpectedly and can be just as powerful as that first shock.

I have days when I feel pretty steady. Days when I can think of you and smile as a memory flows through the projector in my brain. Days when I can tell your story without feeling that jolt of reality hit my piece of earth. Days when I can enjoy the warmth of the sun on my face as I remember our talks on the beach. Days I see your smiling face as a breeze blows my hair gently across my cheek as if a kiss is coming from heaven. I treasure those days. Those are the days I feel like I will survive even when the aftershocks hit.

Just when I'm feeling the illusion of joy, I feel the shift. Some days the jolt hits as my eyes open and reality is there waiting for me. My brain starts screaming, *he is dead. Matt really died.*

Its then when the aftershock throws me off balance.

I see the cracks opening in the earth beneath my feet. I catch my breath as I try to navigate through the rubble that was once my heart. The immense power of the aftershock of reality put me on unstable ground and leaves me questioning whether I'll survive the next one.

I want to scream. I want to punch. I just want not to be. I want to disappear. I want to run as far away as I can. To leave this unstable ground and find a safe place to dwell. I want my ground not to shift on a dime. I want to walk on a steady path, not this twisted, shattered piece of earth.

There are days when the aftershocks leave me paralyzed as I try to navigate an escape. Days when the grief is relentless and nothing I do helps erase the pain.

What I once thought about life has now shifted. I used to think life would go according to my plans. Every belief has started to crack as I continue to live with your loss. All my hopes and dreams fell through the earth and have disappeared from my life forever.

Aftershocks have been noted to sometimes be more dangerous and damaging than the original earthquake. I once thought that had to be a falsehood. But as I continue to live through years of aftershocks, I realize they are far more powerful than the original assault.

The aftershocks are constant reminders that my ground will never go back to what it once was. That I will always be at risk for an aftershock to hit and knock me off my feet. That my terrain will always be full of fault lines and my grief will find a way through.

Grief and aftershocks have a lot in common. We are never given a warning. They hit. Making us unstable. Shaking our once steady world changing the way we look at life.

Like grief, aftershocks can be deep or close to our surface. What matters most is that we recognize them when they hit. We stop and feel them. We allow ourselves to be where we need to be as the earth shifts. We allow ourselves the time to learn how to navigate through our fault lines.

Lessons I've learned from grief

Matt,

I never wanted to have this personal relationship with grief that I do. I never thought I would know this heartbreaking, life-changing type of grief. I never thought it would become my life partner. I never thought it would become a part of my soul and stay forever in my heart. This grief is like the blood that pumps through my body. It has become part of who I am.

I've learned that grief doesn't keep track of time. Although four years have passed since your death, this grief is as powerful as it was in the very beginning. I've learned that the first year is not the hardest. Surviving all those firsts really means nothing. That first-year fog protects you like a warm cocoon. It shields you from the reality that life will never be the same. It enables you to continue to breathe, to survive. But in no way does it prepare you for what is to come.

I've learned that this grief does not soften with the passing of time. I've learned there is no escape from those unexpected gut-punches. Those powerful, crushing waves continue to knock me off balance just as they did in the very beginning.

Time brings with it the harsh reality that this is it. This grief is here to stay. This grief remains as overpowering and relentless, showing no signs of letting up. Time continues to march on as years follow, dragging me through the next birthday and holiday without you. Dragging me kicking and screaming, begging for a short break from the pain of your loss.

I've learned there are no stages of grief. I bounce from one emotion to the next without warning. There are no straight set of rules. There is no passing one stage to get to another. No passing Go to find peace.

Grief is not linear. Grief is a tangled mess. The more you fight the emotions, the tighter its grip becomes on your heart. Grief is anxious and dirty. Grief is losing control in the blink of an eye. Grief is a trigger that hits like an explosion in your head and heart. Grief is the mess your life becomes after losing a child.

I've learned grief never sleeps. She's there lurking in every corner waiting to pounce as soon as she feels your vulnerability surface. Grief grabs you as soon as you awaken and follows you through your day. Like a lost pup, she nips tiny bites at your heels with a sharpness that can't be ignored. Grief follows as you close your eyes to rest. She comes in those haunting memories, the what-ifs, the should-haves, the whys. Grief is a 24/7 animal.

I've learned that grief can partner with guilt, adding regret for things done, said, not done and not said. She teams up with so many powerful emotions that leave the heart and soul spinning out of control. Grief is a constant reminder of reality. Grief continues to beat you down until you are battered and bruised. Grief—however long she's been in your life—will continue to take your breath away.

I've learned that grief will shake your beliefs about God. I questioned why he allowed you to die. I questioned why my prayers for keeping you safe were ignored. I questioned where God was when you were taking your last breath. I questioned where he is now.

I've learned that without God, I would never have survived your death. I've learned that God is quiet and I need to let him be in control. I've learned that what happened in your life and at the time of your death was between you and God. I've learned to talk to God like he is a friend, not always in a prayer but like he is standing beside me. I've learned that if I open myself up to signs they will be there.

I've learned that I'll never be the same woman. The eyes looking back at me show a profound sadness. I've learned that I have an inner strength I never knew existed. I fear nothing.

I've learned never to take life for granted. I appreciate the sunrise, the birds singing, the warmth of a winter sun. I look at life through a different lens. I judge less. I've learned everyone is living through something hidden behind the masks we wear.

I've learned that living with grief is not for the faint of heart. I've learned my grief has a life of its own. I know there is no escape. I've learned my grief must be accepted and acknowledged. My grief is as powerful as my love was and remains for you. I've learned not to fight when the waves hit. I must allow the grief to wash over me, knowing that my life will always be vulnerable to those little things that bring you back to me.

The future that was never meant to be

Matt,

I'm having such a hard time believing that we are coming up on fifty months. The third of March marks another month added to the long list of the months that have passed since your death. I find myself feeling guilty and anxious that I've not been able to follow that so-called grief path. Society continues to believe that grief comes with an expiration date. I find this disturbing, as it makes me feel like there really is something wrong with me.

I'm tired of trying to talk myself into feeling better, like I should be able to adjust to life without my youngest son like someone adjusts to a change in the weather. As if enough time will ever pass to make me less vulnerable to those grief waves.

Those who have never experienced child loss have no idea how life-altering and complicated our grief truly is. I've seen the look on people's faces when I tell your story and begin to choke up. I've heard, "Oh, I thought it just happened recently, not four years ago."

As if a mother should put on the stiff upper lip as she speaks about her dead child.

I tell those who've never buried a child that this experience is similar to childbirth. One can tell you how it feels and what might be expected but until you experience it on a personal level, you will never come close to imagining how those contractions can take you to a place of excruciating pain almost unimaginable to the human mind. The pain of child loss does the same.

As childbirth comes with hopes and dreams for the future, child loss comes with the demolition of those dreams. That's the worst part of a parent's grief. Not only have we lost our child, we've also lost their future. In losing that future, we have lost a large part of ourselves.

That's the biggest misconception society will never understand. When a parent buries their child, they bury so much more. Child loss goes against what society deems as normal. Children are supposed to bury their parents, not the other way around. That is the so-called norm we're taught to believe from childhood. I stressed about how you would survive after I died. Never once did I think I would be the one struggling to survive after your death.

You will be forever thirty-seven. Your future cut brutally short. The dreams of what I desperately wanted for you died with you and left me struggling to accept that your future was never meant to be. Those dreams of watching you take a bride. Of receiving a call that your son or daughter had arrived. Watching you experience fatherhood. Or watching you grow old and gray, and still want to walk on the beach with your mom.

Child loss is like none other. Parents like me remain unnamed. We're not widows, nor are we orphans. The English language has yet to identify a word to describe us.

Losing a child is absolutely indescribable.

The length of time after child loss makes no difference. It's new each day as parents wake and reality hits. Our brains and bodies have the grueling task of moving into the future as we leave a part of our hearts behind.

Arriving at the train station in Washington, D.C.
for my first Fed Up rally in October 2015.

The struggle is real

Matt,

I find it shocking how those waves of emotion can hit and cause me to crash back into that dark, angry place. My mind continues to battle anxiety, grief, and guilt. I feel like a juggler, trying to keep those emotions high in the air, far away from my heart. Life is different now. Time has done nothing to lessen the reality that continues to send shock waves through my soul.

This grief is like none other. I continue to tell myself that this is my new reality. That you really did die. It's like my brain knows the truth but continues to put up that barrier protecting my sanity.

My body's taken a hit. When the memory of hearing those painful words replay in my brain, my throat starts to constrict. My heart starts to race and my stomach turns inside out. There are days I feel like I'm silently dying, that little by little my body is slowly disengaging from life. I feel like I've been knocked senseless. There are days I feel like I'm losing my mind.

Memories are so bittersweet. Flashes of your smiling face, images of you walking on the beach with the dogs continue to take my breath away. I want so badly to reach out and touch your skin. To see you turn around and open your arms to me. I want to wake up from this nightmare and hug you. I want to be transported back in time.

I struggle trying to make sense of what I never saw coming. Why would a parent ever think they would outlive their child? My worry was how you would fare if something happened to me. Now I touch your urn and force my heart to accept that this is all that's left of your beautiful face, your amazing eyes, your contagious laugh and your heartwarming smile.

I struggle with my faith, my belief in heaven, my hope of seeing you again. Of never again being separated by death. I continue to question why God allowed you to die. Is it punishment for something I've said or done? Was your death at thirty-seven already predestined at your birth? So many unanswered questions haunt me as I lay in bed enveloped in the darkness of my grief.

I struggle with society's perception of how long grief should last. I question myself. It's been four years and two months yet it continues to hurt like hell and feel like yesterday.

I feel like I'm starring in Groundhog Day, reliving your death every morning as I remember I can't pick up the phone and hear your voice. We can't share what's been happening in our day. I relive it every night as I drag my exhausted mind into bed, realizing I haven't wished you a peaceful night.

I search for books written by other grieving parents, looking for answers on how to survive this devastating loss. I've found we all share the common bonds of shock, numbness, and despair. That others like me share the feeling of losing their minds over the unthinkable loss of their child. Like me, their bodies and brains have taken a hit. That life will never return to normal.

We all live in the reality of before and after. We've learned that everything we thought we knew about grief was a lie. It knows no boundaries. It has no timeline. It hits hard when least expected. It moves in and never leaves.

I struggle with friends who are no longer. Those who chose to walk away as if my grief was a virus they needed protection from. Fellow nurses whose ups and downs I've shared, holding them up as they buried husbands, celebrating marriages and grandchildren. Giving me one last hug at your funeral and disappearing into the sunset.

I struggle with the disappearance of family members. Life is just too busy for a visit or phone call. Those I thought would have become closer have drifted away. I've learned we are not promised tomorrow. I was one of them before your death. Always thinking there was time to make that call or plan a visit.

I struggle to lower my expectations of people. I struggle with the reality that along with you, I've lost many more.

I struggle with expectations of myself, who I am and what I must do to survive the rest of my life. I struggle accepting that I had no say in how life would be. I struggle with self-kindness and care. I struggle with giving myself permission to throw my mask against the wall and allow the world to see the real me.

I struggle with cutting myself a break when I realize that tears flow at a moment's notice with no warning as to why.

Then I remember. I lost my son.

I have earned the right to scream if I need to. I've earned the right to take a step back and hold onto whatever or whoever is throwing a life preserver my way. I've earned the right to be pissed at the world. To be pissed at people who complain about their lives on days when reminders of you are everywhere.

Most of all, I've accepted that my struggle to find peace will continue for a lifetime. As will my longing to see you again.

Grief is like a jar of pickles

Matt,

Since your death, I've been living not just with complicated grief, but also with PTSD, posttraumatic stress disorder. There are days when the slightest noise has me hanging from the ceiling. I struggle with not knowing where I fit in anymore. There are days when I question my role here on earth. Your addiction kept me crazy, but your death left me broken and questioning life.

The old me left the day you did, and the new me struggles with who I'm supposed to be now. It feels like being transported to another place where you don't understand the language. You constantly get lost and find yourself looking for something familiar.

I've learned that very few people understand when I try to explain what it's like to be me. They think I should be back to my pre-grief state. That life should just return to normal and drag me with it. What they don't and never will understand is that profound loss slices you in half. You become the *before* and the *after* pieces of your tragedy. As time passes, the before you drifts further and further away. Leaving you with an identity that even you can't identify with. You long for the old you but know the road back to finding her again has imploded.

I find it harder and harder to remember the woman I was before your death. The girl who laughed at the stupidest of things. Who would even laugh at herself. I remember looking forward to little things. I remember having happy hours and bonfires. I remember having lots of fun. I remember a reflection with bright eyes and a natural smile. Now I see a silhouette slowly drifting away in a fog.

Trauma changes you. It unravels you. It takes you to the darkest places. Things you once thought would never happen have happened, leaving you hanging from that mental cliff, clinging to the last piece of your soul. The old you has been sucked away, and the new you lay in pieces at your feet. You try to make sense of this, but the pieces are hard to fit together like a puzzle that just doesn't make sense when a large piece is missing.

I was with a friend one day. This friend totally gets where I'm coming from. She understands when I say the old me has vanished and this new me is still struggling to fit like a pair of old jeans that once felt like home, now rewoven and uncomfortable.

She has survived her own trauma. The assault of breast cancer on her body and mind. Like me, the *before* her was totally destroyed and replaced with an *after* person she continues to try to identify with.

We both grieve the women we once were, and often compare notes on how things continue to have a trickledown effect on both our lives. During one of these conversations she said something that gave me an ah-ha moment, putting a true perspective on what I've been living with since your death. Without even knowing how profound this statement was and how it would impact me for the rest of my life, she calmly looked me in the eye and said, "Once you become a pickle, you can never go back to being a cucumber."

Yes, I know it sounds like a crazy thing to say in the midst of an emotional conversation. But when you really think about it, it's the most insightful statement I've ever heard about who you become after living with grief or surviving trauma. The transformation from cucumber to pickle can never be reversed. Everything used in the process leaves a permanent mark. The same with grief, whether it's over the loss of a child or the loss of a healthy you, it leads you through a process that can never be undone.

There are days when the world can be sweet but suddenly, without warning, an unexpected trigger can turn everything dark. Just like a jar of pickles, we never know how the day will taste. Will it leave us with an unpleasant bitterness or a fleeting moment of unexpected pleasure? We never know how the aftereffects of grief will play out as we navigate unfamiliar territory.

It continues to amaze and comfort me that a simple statement had the power to validate what I feel on a daily basis. It also brings me comfort knowing that I'm not the only pickle trying to find my place in the glass jar called life.

Matt with the love of his life, Natalie, on the bay in Lewes, Delaware.

Believing while I'm grieving

Matt,

Since your death, my faith has taken a beating. I was so numb that first year, my brain didn't have the capacity to grasp that your death was reality. My foggy brain refused to let that reality break through the steel cocoon that kept me sane and surviving all those firsts.

As the years have passed, I now find myself in a constant state of anxiety wondering about the afterlife. I remember praying for God to keep you safe when you moved to Florida for treatment. I prayed day and night that you would survive your disease and find your way to recovery. When you died, I questioned if God ever heard my prayers or if God saw the big picture and saved you the only way he could.

I continue to search for answers. I scan the internet for articles written by those who survived a near-death experience. Those who speak about seeing their bodies floating above the accident scene or surgical suite. Those who speak about feeling peaceful and experienceing a joy they never knew here on earth. Of bright lights, glorious flowers, and beautiful voices. Of being welcomed by beings they felt an immediate kinship with. Of never being afraid.

My bookshelf holds books by doctors and experts on near-death experiences. I feel like I'm walking through the desert dying of thirst, and trying to quench this thirst by reading everything I can find to help my heart accept that you are in a better place. I continue to search for anything that will give my heart hope.

The one book I never opened was my Bible. It remained on my nightstand untouched. I don't know if I was mad at God or just didn't trust him anymore. A part of me felt He either didn't hear my prayers to keep you safe or He chose to ignore them. Every conversation I've had with God since your death ends with me saying to God that we must agree to disagree. I wanted you saved on earth. Obviously, God had other plans.

One day while searching the internet I found a reference on death, and life after death. To my surprise that piece was referencing the Bible. I was having one of those very dark days when grief was overwhelming my soul. I felt like I wasn't going to make it through the day. The reality that you were gone and I would never see you again on this earth was just too painful for me to accept. On that day, I reached for that book I had ignored for so long and began to read.

I found the passages that were referenced in my internet search. Before I knew what was happening, I started to feel a slight sense of peace. The more I read, the more I wanted to read. I can't explain what happened to me as I read those words written over two-thousand years ago, but I know I felt a shift in my soul.

Everything I'd been searching for all these years was right here. Everything I needed to know about where you were had been sitting untouched on my nightstand. My Bible has become my go-to book. I know you are probably laughing at me, but it's true. I read the Bible every morning and continue to find a peace that baffles even me.

My favorite verse is in the book of John. One my bad days I sit by myself and let those words wash over me. John 14 gives me hope that you are with Jesus, and one day I will be there with you.

> *Let not your hearts be trouble*. *Believe in Go*, *believe also in me. In my Father's house are many rooms. If it were no so, woul* I *have tol* you that I go to prepare a place for you? An* if I go an* prepare a place for you, I will come again an* will take you to myself, that where I am you may be also.*

I'm not going to lie. I still have those days when I question why God didn't save you the way I wanted him to. I still have days when my anxiety gets the best of me. I still tell God we will continue to agree to disagree about your death, but I also have days where I feel a peace come over me as I read those words written so long ago.

I remember sitting on the beach together. We both loved the beach so much. I remember laying back looking at the blue sky and saying heaven is a beach. I remember you laughing and saying, "I hope so, Mom."

Matt, I hope so too. I hope when it's my time, I will wake up on a beach and see you running toward me. Until then I hold onto John 14, and slowly begin to rekindle my faith.

They said time would heal the pain

Matt,

Today is Mother's Day. My fifth without you. Even as I write these words I still struggle with my reality. The thought that you really aren't coming through my door with flowers in your hand and a dog at your heel continues to break my heart.

How did we get here? I still question why you left, why life turned out to be this nightmare. Why God didn't answer my prayers like I wanted. You should be here.

Today is such an incredibly painful day. For weeks I've been tortured by the Hallmark commercials with smiling moms and beautiful children. The perfect family gathered around the perfect mother celebrating their perfect day.

Doesn't Hallmark know that for some, Mother's Day is a brutal reminder of what we no longer have? Of children who no longer live?

Children who won't be calling or sending cards to celebrate our day? Children whose voices were silenced by an untimely death? Children whose faces and smiles are frozen in time?

Mother's Day was once a day I looked forward to. If my love was enough, you would be sitting beside me surrounded by family. We would be laughing and hugging. Filling our plates with crabs and corn, sharing stories of your childhood antics with your brother. Pups would be chasing squirrels as we enjoyed the beauty of my gardens and the warmth of the shining sun.

Today all I have are precious memories and cards from past Mother's Day. Treasured pieces of paper signed by you. I hold them close, reading each word while running my finger over your signature. You always laughed at me for saving cards. Perhaps now you understand why.

Today there is no family gathering. No shining sun. Today, the weather mimics my soul. Dreary and cold. Rain hitting the window makes me think that the angels are crying for moms like me. Knowing this pain will never let go. I will mourn you as long as I breathe.

Today I will give myself a gift. I will allow memories to overflow in my mind as tears fall shamelessly from my eyes. I will not pretend to be okay. The mask I wear to get through life will remain in hiding.

Today I will be true to my grief. I will allow it to wrap its arms around my soul as I remember you as my loving son. Today I will allow myself to break. I will close my eyes and see your smiling face.

Today I will reaffirm that I will always be your mother. I pray I will feel you with me. That you will be with me in spirit as I remember your love as both my little boy and as an amazing man. I will speak to you as if you were sitting next to me. I will pray for a sign showing me you are near.

Today I will be that mother learning to survive her day. A mother learning to live with a broken heart on her special day. A mother living with a child who lives in heaven.

Marching alongside thousands of grieving families in Washington, D.C.

Memorial Day memories

Matt,

Today is Memorial Day. The day is bright and beautiful. White puffy clouds dot the blue sky. A hint of a breeze stirs the treetops. Memories are flooding my mind this morning as I sit on the deck listening to the birds sing. Memories of happy times before you left. Memories of sun and sand. Dogs running through the surf while you and I enjoyed the warmth of the sun on our pale winter skin.

Closing my eyes, I can hear your voice. You hated the beginning of the summer season. The noise, the crowds. You complained that the tourists invaded your piece of heaven. I can see that scowl on your face as you contemplated your way to the sea while fighting through hours of traffic.

The summer season was upon your precious, peaceful place and you had little tolerance for the hustle and bustle those crowds brought to your sleepy little beach town.

I remember you pacing as you grabbed leashes that would now be required when we walked the dogs. Days of running free on the beach had come to a screeching halt. I could see their eyes questioning what you're doing as you leashed them up and headed out your door.

I remember walking with you to the bay as we moved from one side of the street to the other to avoid the golf carts driving through the once quiet streets of town. I knew better than to try to bring you out of your funk. Grabbing your hand, I reminded you of times not too long ago when I was the one complaining of the noise while you were enjoying being part of the beach crowds. As you matured, we blended together in our dislike of noise and crowds.

Those were the days we would escape to the sea. Packing the cooler with plenty of ice for the dogs, we would head out for the day. I was in awe of your ability to control such a powerful machine. You became one with your boat. I could see your face begin to relax as the seaspray hit and we bounced over the waves. Your laughter was music to my ears.

So many lazy days were spent away from the noise. You would anchor us as I watched you become one with the sea. You would spot a school of dolphins and jump in while I stood back watching trying to keep the dogs from joining your party. You taught me not to fear life, but to embrace it. So many great conversations were shared as we sat together floating on the bluest of seas under the warm sun.

Today my heart grows heavy as I remember those precious times together. My heart refusing to think they would ever end. Years have passed since we shared our Memorial Day tradition of escaping the crowds to spend the day in our peaceful place.

Both your precious boat and you, my precious son, are gone. I am left to remember and grieve the loss of times that are never to be again. I always think of you as I look out at the vastness of the ocean. Closing my eyes I can see you standing at the wheel, the seaspray hitting your face as your laughter dances in my heart.

Matt

Father's Day fantasies, again

Matt,

Tomorrow is Father's Day. It's the first Father's Day since your death that we'll be having what used to be our traditional family crab feast. Except this time it's only going to be your brother, Heather, and Maddie who will be here with us.

Since your death, special days are just too painful to continue the traditions of the past. Your absence leaves a huge void in what used to be a happy time together. There is no avoiding the empty space your death left behind.

Even after four years, my mind still slips into denial, allowing me to fool myself and pretend you are just away. Knowing that reality is just too painful to bear, I fantasize what life would be like today had you survived your disease.

I picture you with a little girl. A towheaded beauty. With the most amazing green eyes and crooked smile. You would come bouncing in like you always did, and she would be riding on your shoulders squealing with joy. Of course a black lab would be in hot pursuit of the giggling girl.

You would greet me with a kiss and wrap me in that big bearhug while your girl wiggled away and ran to greet her Uncle Mike. I picture my two boys, now men hitting each other on the back and sharing your famous, "Hey, Bro."

You would be grabbing a crab out of the pile and chasing the kids around the table. You were always the prankster even as a grown man. We would gather outside and share the happenings of our lives. Laughter and love would envelope us like the rays of the sun as we shared the bond of being a close-knit family.

I picture the kids and dogs chasing each other through the garden, laughter mingling with barking as we tried to regain a semblance of control. Seeing my boys and their families together for a day to celebrate fatherhood would have been a dream come true for me. You would have been an amazing father. You were such a loving uncle to Maddie.

Sadly, I will never live that dream. You are gone and there is no little towhead for me to love. No wife, no child here for me to hold onto. No child who has your beautiful eyes for me to gaze into and find you. You took it all when you left. All I have is deep unrelenting grief on what could have been and what is.

There are no words to explain how losing you is losing me. All the hopes and dreams I once had for us shattered into pieces that will never fit together again.

Tomorrow I will think of you as I watch your brother and his beautiful daughter. I will imagine you walking through my door. I will close my eyes and see your smiling face.

I will always long for one more hug. One more, "Hey, Mom." One more day of having my sons together.

Matt with his brother Mike and niece Madison after a day of crabbing.

Matt with my husband Ray at our wedding reception.

It's not the firsts that kill you

Matt,

I'm still feeling the aftershocks of your death. Four years later I still find myself on shaky, unstable ground. I flip from acceptance as if I have any choice, to a blatant denial that your addiction ended your life and my dreams for your future.

I still find myself beating back a rage that I thought had become a little softer. Oh, how wrong I was. This rage grips my soul. Makes me want to lash out and scream until my lungs are void of air. I want to shake my fist toward the heavens and demand answers. I want God to show his face and help me understand why my heart, though shattered into jagged little pieces, continues to beat.

Everything about grief is a blatant lie. I've read that if you just make it through all the firsts, life suddenly will take an upward swing. Like winning an unexpected lottery. Wow, the firsts I've found were the easiest to survive. My brain remained in shock, shrouded by that protective impenetrable fog. Keeping my heart and soul enclosed in a tight barrier that nothing could touch.

I walked around in a daze. Numb to what was happening around me. Denial became my constant companion. I could not even allow myself to think that your addiction won.

Slowly as the years continued, the fog started to lift. The barrier began to crumble and reality began to slap my face on a daily basis. The pain that was once living at a safe distance hit my heart like a well-aimed arrow piercing what was left of my soul.

Society believes that time heals all wounds. The only thing time does for grief is give it a powerful grip over your soul. The passing years bring new triggers. I'm still shocked by the force of gut-punches I feel when memories hit out of the blue.

I still choke as I walk by a bag of salt-and-vinegar chips. I still face an internal battle as I walk down the deodorant aisle and see a stick of Axe sitting innocently on the store shelf. I battle touching the bottle. Lifting the lid and taking in your favorite scent. I hear your voice asking me to look for the Phoenix scent if I was going shopping. I can't explain this guttural reaction to a stranger as unexpected sobs fill the aisle when I remove the lid and allow myself a moment to remember. To smell a scent that is you.

After four years I'm still learning to navigate shaky ground. Land mines are everywhere. These passing years continue to be filled with aftershocks from the first days my world imploded under my feet.

Some days I can feel them coming. Birthdays, holidays and anniversary dates cause my body to react with physical pain. I am shaking and breathless knowing that even after surviving those firsts, it's the years coming that will continue to bring me to the edge of my dark abyss. Threatening what little piece of sanity I've somehow managed to maintain.

I now understand that grief has no time limit. It has a mind of its own. It has no logic or compassion. It hurts like hell and no amount of passing time will ease the pain that has a death grip on my soul.

It strikes without warning. It's the most powerful, misunderstood emotion known in this life. I also understand why society lies about grief. If we knew the truth we would choose not to exist.

As time passes, I continue to wonder what you would look like. What you would be doing with your life. Questions that will never have answers continue to haunt my reality. Losing you was losing a big piece of me. Your future was also mine. A daughter-in-law, more babies to give my heart joy. Your death was not yours alone.

I'm learning that my grieving you will never be completed. I will never get over it. There will be no closure. The aftershocks and reality slaps will continue to find me. Some expected, some out of the blue. My anger will ebb and flow. Rearing its ugly head at the injustice of how your life's pages were ripped from the book that should have held so many more chapters

A gift from a mother who knew my grief. We both felt that
the book of our children's lives had closed too soon.

Collateral beauty of shared grief

Matt,

One definition of collateral beauty is beauty that is impossible to see. Perhaps a devastating tragedy has broken your life beyond repair. This tragedy so unimaginable, so incomprehensible, has rendered you powerless to see beyond your brokenness.

This weekend I witnessed the recurring presence of collateral beauty as I attended The Compassionate Friends national conference in Philadelphia.

This conference was specifically for parents like me. Parents who have survived the unsurvivable. We have outlived our children. We have received the phone call that no parent could ever imagine receiving. We have heard those words, "Your child is dead."

We know what it's like to try to breathe after our hearts have been ripped from our chests and lay shattered at our feet. We know the pain of planning a celebration of life when we should have been planning a birthday, a family barbecue, a wedding.

I really had no idea what to expect. I could feel anxiety gripping my throat as I stood in line waiting for the conference materials. I remember looking around and recognizing the pain etched on parents who knew my grief. We were each given a red lanyard with our names displayed for everyone to see. Many like me carried pictures of beautiful smiling faces. Faces that should be here. Faces that should be laughing and living. Faces not memorialized but alive and well.

My heart began to race. My twisted thoughts gripped my brain. I wanted to scream. Hey! Do you really think we need to wear a lanyard? Look at our faces. Look at our eyes. Grief has been etched permanently into our being. All you need to do is look. We are marked by unimaginable loss.

I remember walking into the ballroom and scanning the room. I could feel my tears beginning as I found the nearest table. So many people gathered together, it was as though we were one broken soul encompassing every inch of available space. No longer strangers. No shame, no uneasiness. Our connection was palpable. Pictures, names, and stories were shared without one thought of judgement or guilt.

Conversations that are taboo in society flowed like nectar from an exquisite flower. Nothing was off limits. The timeframe of our losses was never an issue. The cause of death was shared without the worry of judgement. The reality that our child died overrode the hows or the whys. These parents understand that this life-altering grief will last a lifetime.

Unlike society's perception of grief having a timetable with stages that lead to the completion of mourning, these parents recognize that loss of a child is neither linear nor logical. It's layered with secondary losses. We have not just lost a child. We have lost the present and the future. We have lost hopes and dreams.

During this amazing time, I never felt the need to defend my grief. I never felt the awkwardness I've felt among those who feel that enough time has passed and I should be over Matt's death. I felt connected to those who needed no explanation when my tears flowed and my sobs echoed across the crowded room.

Mothers I've come to know and love due to the power of social media showed me compassion and comfort. Hugs and tears mingled as we were finally able to physically wrap our arms around each other, knowing that nothing need be said. We live it. We get it.

I was given the gift of just being Matt's mom. I was given permission to leave my mask behind. To let my advocacy have a few days off. To disappear into and acknowledge my son and the sorrow of the profound loss I live with everyday. Permission to mourn is the greatest gift we can ever give to another bereaved parent.

I silently watched as collateral beauty surrounded me. I witnessed it as parents who were once strangers came together and carried each other's grief. Just for an incredible moment, our grief was lifted by another, allowing our hearts to see the beauty of compassion and understanding that defies explanation.

Collateral beauty shined a light through the dark, the darkness of our brokenness. A light I will carry with me as I continue to live my grief. The experience of catching that glimpse of beauty among the dark ashes of child loss will remain in my heart forever.

A birthday letter

Matt,

Today would have been your forty-second birthday. I should be on my way to the beach to spend time with you on your special day. You and I would spend time together on the beach, taking the dogs and watching their joy as they ran through the surf while we caught up on the happenings in our lives. We would be planning our dinner feast of crabs, shrimp, and beer. We would be heading to JD Shuckers, your favorite restaurant. Our family would be together at our happy place to celebrate you.

But today our reality is much different from my dreams for your birthday. For you are forever thirty-seven, and this is your fifth birthday in heaven. 💔

Today I will spend the morning letting my grief pour out from my soul. Looking through every album I own with pictures of our life.

Beautiful memories of a life with two boys who were always together. Boys staring back at the camera with innocent, beautiful faces. You with your green eyes and Mike with his blue eyes.

Pictures of you with that smile and those beautiful eyes staring back at me through all the phases of your life. Pictures that prove you lived. Beautiful memories of your life from infancy through adulthood. So happy and healthy. It's so hard for me to understand reality. My brain knows you are gone. My heart struggles with the truth.

Today there will be no family party. No cake, no funny card. I will never see you with your brother standing side by side laughing about how you're both over the big four-oh.

Brothers' laughter blending together as you tell stories of childhood antics that mom should never know. Sharing your accomplishments in life as your children listen at your feet.

Your brother Mike will never know the joy of being an uncle. He will never know the joy of holding his brother's children in his arms or teaching them to run through the surf with you by his side. He will never watch his younger brother discover the joys and heartbreaks of being a father.

Mike will never have the opportunity to take your son fishing or show your daughter treasures saved from your childhood. He will never be able to offer advice or share his list of dos and don'ts of fatherhood. There will be no more children squealing with joy as that new puppy comes running into their arms. No more brothers sharing the secret of what makes a house a home.

No more pictures of my boys with arms wrapped over the other's shoulder. No more memories of happy times as we celebrate you growing older. No more handsome faces staring back at the camera telling me to stop with the pictures already. No more blended laughter for your mother to hear.

Losing you is losing a future of love, laughter and beautiful memories. Losing you has left an undeniable void in our lives. Losing you is never seeing my boys together again. Never hearing your laughter as you tell your children stories about your childhood sharing secrets that only your brother would know. Losing you is never dancing at your wedding. Losing you is never sharing the joy of holding your newborn child for the first time. Losing you has split my life into the before and after.

Pictures of myself before your death are almost unrecognizable to me. A real smile. Similar green eyes staring back at the camera. Happiness shining through every photo.

Today, my pictures reflect an emptiness in my eyes. A forced smile. A face broken by grief. Pictures of before and after tell the story of how grief changed me from the inside out. Pictures showing a shadow of who I used to be.

Reality is that I will never see you coming through my door with your children in tow. That smile and those eyes forever gone. No mini Matts for me to spoil and hug. No future generation to share stories of your childhood antics. No more of you. 😢

How I wish heaven had visiting hours just for these special days. I would throw myself into your arms and never let you go. I would tell you how much your loss has changed my life. I would tell you over and over again how much I love you.

I would beg you to stay with me forever.

Today I will honor your life. I will let my grief have its way. Today I will let my tears flow, no longer fighting or pretending that I'm okay. Today I will remember the joy you brought to my life. I will allow myself the gift to grieve. To feel the profound loss of your death.

Today I will close my eyes and remember your hugs, your voice, your smile. I will remember two boys chasing each other through the surf, throwing wet sand as your laughter was carried by the ocean breeze. Today I will accept the reality of knowing that I will grieve for what should have been for the rest of my life.

Happy birthday my beautiful boy. May you celebrate by dancing on the stars and swinging from the moon. May you fly free knowing you are forever in my heart.

Two life-changing words

Matt,

I feel like I've stepped back in time. I never thought that feeling of shocked numbness would ever hit me again like it did after hearing those two words, "Matt's Dead."

We've all heard how one phone call can change the course of your life. Once again knocking you off balance and forcing you to navigate your life on shaky, unrecognizable ground.

I remember those early days after your death. Walking around numb. Feeling like my insides were jelly. Constantly shaking. Walking through the days going through the motions of living, but really not living. I remember the feeling of nothingness. Of denying this was my new reality. Of feeling foolish for sweating the meaningless small stuff that life constantly throws your way. I now knew that life was too fragile to sweat over issues that, in reality, really didn't matter.

Your death was a lesson in my life.

I foolishly believed that after four long years, I was back in control of my life. My advocacy work allowed me to channel my grief into helping others. I finally felt a purpose. I still grieve you every day but felt like as long as I had my advocacy, your death would always have meaning.

I'm still trying to understand where I am today. Whether it was a God intervention or a Matt intervention, I remember the day perfectly. Reliving every step I took. Every thought I had was exactly the same as I experienced upon hearing you were gone.

A beautiful day, June 22. The humidity finally broke and I wanted to fill the house with the cleansing breeze of fresh air. You remember how I always hated having the house closed up. We used to laugh as I would only put the air on when the dogs were getting too hot. I needed to hear the songs of my garden birds. Needed to hear the soothing sounds of the waterfall in the garden beneath the kitchen window.

I lifted the window. It stuck. Instead of giving up, I continued to push as hard as I could. Then pain. It was excruciating. It felt like my back and leg had been stripped of muscle. My nursing instincts kicking in and I hobbled to the freezer. Ice now. I grabbed the bottle of Motrin, swallowed quickly and hobbled to the couch. I sat in shock, looking at the window with such contempt. If I could have, I would have grabbed a hammer and beat the crap out of that piece of glass.

Weeks passed. The pain remained, fueling hate for that window. In my mind it had ruined my summer. No more biking, hiking, dog walking, yoga, gardening. Everything I loved gone in a split second. All my selfcare practices that kept me sane on those dark days now out of my physical capacity.

After two months of continued pain, an MRI was ordered. I was expecting a herniated disc. I was fully prepared to inform which ever neurosurgeon I would see that surgery would be my last resort. After watching how your surgery did nothing for your back except lead you to the road that finally took your life, I was perfecting my speech.

Never in a million years did I see what was coming. You always laughed at me being the health nut. Skipping cake, not eating red meat. I can hear your words so clearly now. *Mom, life's too short. Eat the cake.*

Although the two words were different, their impact on my life was the same.

Fracture. Tumor.

I had the same feeling I did after hearing those other two words, "Matt's dead."

The feeling of leaving my body as my brain searched for that protective cocoon to wrap myself in.

Fracture. Tumor.

Today, I am fighting another reality I never imagined. The reality that I will now be fighting for my life as I fought for yours.

I lie awake in the dark praying for peace as I did many nights after your death. I wake, breathless and shaky. This reality hits just as the reality of your death did. New every morning.

Today I am once again going through the motions numb to where this journey will lead me.

Looking back, that sticking window was a gift. A divine intervention. My doctor calls it an incidental finding because I have no cancer symptoms. I feel fine. If not for the back injury, I would be biking, gardening, and living life unaware of the cancer inside me.

Today, I see light shining through that window. I hear the birds singing and the sounds of soothing water. I watch the dogs chase each other through the gardens. I look at that window and see your beautiful smile. You and God worked together for whatever reason to bring this to my attention. Perhaps my advocacy work isn't over. I promised as long as I lived, you would continue to live.

It's almost ironic. I've always told everyone that losing you was the worst, most devastating event in my life. Surviving your death has taught me that I can survive whatever life chooses to throw my way. Your death was my lesson in how to live.

Matt, walk with me on this new journey. Let me feel you by my side through the biopsies and treatments. Give me signs that you are near. Please thank God for me.

Believe me, I will be eating the cake. I'll take that burger.

I'll remember how you lived and mimic your absolute love for life. I remember you telling me, "Mom, I don't have to worry, you worry enough for us both."

Lesson learned, my beautiful boy. Four years and seven months later your death continues to teach me about life.

Blessings of incidental findings

Matt,

I must admit that when you died, I was so pissed off at God. I felt let down. Abandoned. Like my prayers to keep you safe fell on deaf ears. That my prayers weren't good enough to be answered. God and I had many ugly conversations as I sat in the dark and said things that would have had my grade school nuns running for the holy water to wash out my mouth.

I was shocked at the depth and power of my anger. Growing up in the Catholic church and attending Catholic school, I knew I'd better straighten out my thoughts and get control of my mouth. I dared God to appear to me and explain why he let you die when I prayed you would beat your addiction and recover to live a beautiful life.

I was a spitting mad, grieving mom. Nothing would convince me that Jesus knew what was really happening in your life when I just had my fantasies of how you were living. All I wanted was you back. Under any circumstances. I really didn't care if you were suffering from your disease, I just wanted you back.

I remember going to your garden at our church and sitting under the cross. Seeing your name carved in stone was like another slap from God. Seeing your name, birth date and death date was having my soul ripped from my body and shattered into a million pieces. No mother should ever see her precious child's name on a cold stone.

I took my anger and turned it into an advocacy against those who poisoned you with their pills. I was relentless. I held nothing back. I named names and called people out for who they truly were.

I began helping those who reminded me of you, fighting for them as I fought for you. Four years of advocacy work culminated in six bills that would change how Delaware treats those who suffer from your disease. I surrounded myself with the best advocates Delaware had to offer and channeled my anger into creating a legacy to honor your life.

Little did I know that once again my life would be turned upside down. Looking back, it's really not surprising. My friends kept telling me to take a much needed break. To just enjoy the fact that summer was here and Legislative Hall was out of session. But advocacy is in my blood. Hard to turn it off when people are calling asking for help to find treatment. No way was I not going to do everything in my power to get another mother's son or daughter in a safe place.

Well, it seems that God had another plan for me. Funny how God just decides to take the stubborn bull by the horns and say enough.

I know you know. I have this crazy uncommon cancer. Of course, why not? You and I were always the misfits. Except this time I have no anger against God. I have never felt closer to Jesus in my entire life. It seems Jesus has been beside me all this time. I just ignored him. My grief blocked his peace. My anger did not allow me to feel his presence. He was knocking all along.

Jesus has taken over my care, placed me in the hands of experts. Jesus saved me from the wrong diagnosis. He saved me from an extensive surgery that might not have been the best first step in my fight.

Matt, I know you are here. I feel you and see your smiling face. You gave me such a gift by getting your message to me to fight. You told a friend you still wear your ballcap backwards. You told her about my cancer and my advocacy. You talked about your brother by name. So many messages, I know it's you.

Just like Jesus, you never really left me. I just needed to let my grief open to see the most amazing light shine through. I have a peace like never before. I feel totally confident that Jesus has both of us in the palm of his hand.

Matt, you were always my beautiful boy. Now I know you are my guardian angel. I know that you will be watching from heaven. I know you are at peace, and that's the most beautiful gift I could have received in the middle of my storm.

Blessings continue to find me. Ray is amazing. My friends, those precious few who stood by me after your death, are now carrying me through this new journey.

Blessings totally unexpected, yet so welcomed. I continue to learn from you, my beautiful boy.

I sit and remember our conversations when your wisdom shined though. Believe me Matt, I'm going to enjoy those little things I always overlooked. I see you in the stars, I see you in the sunsets. I know heaven is your beach and you, my son, are enjoying peace by your precious sea.

I will fight for you and my family. Yet when my time comes, meet me by the sea. We'll run through the surf together. You wearing your ballcap backwards and me with my crazy curls. Together forever one day. Godspeed my boy. Tell Jesus your mom says thanks for not giving up on her.

SEPTEMBER 25, 2019

This crazy rollercoaster called life

Matt,

I feel like I did during those days when we battled your addiction. One day when things were going as planned, I felt like I could fly. I was always so hopeful every time you agreed to treatment. Like life would return to normal and you would finally return to the life your addiction stole from you. Well, we all know how that worked out. Your addiction was stronger than my love. It was so conniving and clever, it convinced you that you were in control.

You left this world on January 3, 2015. You were gone forever and my world was changed in the blink of an eye. For years I walked around in a fog. Disbelief and denial became my constant companions.

Just when I was starting to feel like I had a handle on my grief after living the uncharted life of a grieving mother four years and eight months after your death, life once again became a rollercoaster ride.

I was diagnosed with cancer, and the rollercoaster plummeted to the earth. Once again my world was thrust into the unknown. Shock, disbelief, and panic found me again.

Those feelings returned with a vengeance. I walked around numb like I did during your active addiction. All those feelings I had buried came rushing to the surface.

My cancer made your absence even more traumatic. I wondered if you knew what was happening here on earth. I prayed for so long that you would come to me just for a moment to let me know you were okay. Finally finding your peace that eluded you here on earth.

Imagine my joy when I received a message from a friend that you came to her and asked her to get a message to me. You told her you were Matt. You asked her to let me know you still wore your ballcap backwards. You told her it was not my time and I must fight. You told her things only you could know.

Your message meant the world to me. Knowing you were still here was the best gift I could have received. Once again I felt like I could fly. The rollercoaster was going up, up, up. Little did I know that soon enough it would once again crash to the ground.

If I hadn't seen it with my own eyes, I would never have believed Belle attacked Molly for no reason. I immediately called our vet. Belle had started to show signs of aggression that was so not her. Belle was the sweetest dog I'd ever rescued. I thought she was reacting to my stress until the aggression continued to get worse. It got to the point we had to slightly sedate her to make sure the aggression would stop.

I remember the day I felt her head and thought I was going to vomit. We were sitting on the deck and she was rubbing her head on the furniture. I called her over to rub her head, hoping to find the spot that was bothering her. What I felt was a solid mass the size of a golf ball. I panicked. I snapped a picture and sent it to Stephanie, our vet.

The news broke my heart. Belle had a quick growing brain tumor. Her aggression, like your addiction, would take her life. For one week Bella was spoiled. Steak, hamburger, pizza—anything she wanted she got. The thing that was hardest was that emotionally and physically I could not go to the vet with her.

Your brother was so full of compassion. He told me, "Mom it's not physically possible for you to be there. I will be there for you. You know Mike loved Bella as much as I did."

Like you, Mike took to her as soon as I brought her home. We spent many days together with our dogs playing in the surf.

Stephanie was not just our vet. She was my friend for years. She loved Belle as much as we did. I could not have asked for two better people to say goodbye to my dearest friend.

We put if off as long as possible. I had to fight my selfish need to keep her here with me. I spoke to so many of my dog friends who all relieved my guilt for doing the right thing for my beloved companion of fourteen years.

Bella was the one who paced with me at night after your death. Sleep was not something that came easy. She was constantly by my side. Bella was the one who found me in your closet surrounded by your clothing sobbing like a wounded animal. I remember her walking into the closet, lifting her nose and taking in your scent. I could see in her eyes she knew it was you. She kept nudging me with her nose, forcing her body into my lap. She lay there with me for hours, once again licking tears off my face and comforting me with her presence.

Bella left me the day after my birthday. She could hold on no longer. I could not watch her suffer any longer. I prayed you would be there with Kahlua when she crossed the rainbow bridge. Mike said her last act of love was to kiss his face as if saying thank you.

Another tremendous loss. Losing you, now losing another connection to you. The rollercoaster continues to keep my life on unstable ground. Never knowing if I will be soaring toward the sky or crashing to the ground.

I do know I have no control over the ride. I just have to hold on, pray and let Jesus lead the way.

I miss you, I miss me, too

Matt,

I don't know why your monthly anniversary on October 3, hit me so hard. It's been four years and nine months since you left this earth, but for some reason this month's anniversary hit me like a well thrown brick. Perhaps it's because we are only three months short of your fifth year angelversary. My brain knows you have been gone this long, my heart still struggles with this painful reality.

I feel like a broken piece of pottery. Once whole. Once beautiful. Once useful. Now I've been shattered so many times, the pieces that compose me are sharp and jagged. No longer fitting perfectly together. Leaving large gaps that will never fit together to make me whole again.

I look at pictures of us. Smiling faces stare back at me. You as an innocent child in my arms. The joy radiating from my eyes. I look at pictures of you and Mike. Both happy and healthy. Sadly, there will be no more pictures of you. What I have is all that will ever be.

My pictures look nothing like the broken woman I've morphed into. My eyes carry a sadness that can't be disguised. My smile is nothing like the one before your death. Some days I look at my reflection in the mirror and want to cry. I miss who I was before your death.

Now, as I battle cancer, my reflection is even more painful. I look like a ghost of the woman I was before. Pain has taken its toll on my body. Your loss continues to shock and shatter me. The pictures never gave a clue as to how our lives would take a turn that would change me into someone I no longer recognize.

My losses just keep piling on. First your death. Then my career. Next were the friends who ran out of my life as fast as their legs could carry them. Losing both Bella and Simon within weeks of each other was losing another connection to you. Now, it's my health.

I wonder if I'll ever be able to piece myself together again. I wonder if my body will return to a state of normal and allow me to enjoy the little things again. Yoga and biking. Walking the dogs and making dinner. Things I always took for granted, as I took for granted that you would beat your disease and live.

So now I struggle to pick up my pieces and find a way to make them fit. The problem with broken pottery is once it's broken, it can never be repaired to the original state. It will always show the cracks. It will always show signs of damage.

The life I'm left to live is one I never saw coming. I've read that grief consists of two parts. The first being loss. The next is the remaking of life. Funny, life has continued to go on around me.

I am older and somewhat wiser. I have learned not to sweat the small stuff, as so much of life really is small stuff. I have learned to stop and feel my grief. I've forgiven myself for not being able to save you. I know I will never return to the woman I was before your death. I'm trying to rebuild my pieces.

Somedays I remember you, me, and Mike holding hands while singing, "Humpty Dumpty sat on a wall. Humpty Dumpty had a big fall. All the king's horses and all the king's men couldn't put Humpty together again."

Matt, never did I think I would be Humpty. I miss you. I miss me. I miss who we used to be.

Matt with his dog Beau relaxing after a long
walk on the beach in Lewes, Delaware.

The layers of my grief

Matt,

Somedays I feel like I'm layered in grief. I remember how I would layer my clothing on those iffy weather days. Never knowing if the sun would break through the clouds and warm the gloomy day. This grief is heavier than my clothing and, unlike my clothing, cannot be ripped off when the waves hit and the tide recedes.

I feel like an onion. Peeling through the multiple layers will leave you in tears. Whenever I feel I've come to grips with your death, I'm hit by another wave. My tears come as the overwhelming feeling of sinking into the abyss hits like a slap.

My cancer diagnosis has compounded your death. I need you here. I want you here. You should be here. I need to hear your voice telling me, "You got this, Mom." I need you to talk to your brother as only brothers can. I need you to be here to help me face the unknown.

I need you so badly that I feel myself reliving that horrific fresh pain I experienced early after your death.

I grieve what could have been. I grieve who I used to be. I grieve for the life I took for granted. I grieve for Ray and all he has lost in a companion.

Layer after layer after layer, the grief builds up like volcanic ash. Get too close and you get burned. Tears flow like ash completely out of control. Then the flow stops and mountains of ash are left behind. Mountains that block this journey to finding peace. Mountains of tests since my diagnosis. Grief over the possibilities. Mountains of newly woken grief over you not being here to hug me. Grief over how quickly plans and life changes. Grief when I hear your brother's voice begin to crack as we both share our feeling about your absence.

I've read that grieving is a lifelong process. I'll never get over your loss. I'll never get over losing me. I pray for the strength to carry the layers, as my journey through multifaceted grief will continue as long as I live.

Peeling an onion is like dealing with grief one step at a time. The onion comes apart one layer at a time. If you peel harshly you can tear through the layers, causing damage. If you peel gently the layers fall off easily. I'll work to peel gently through my layers. Working through one layer at a time. Dealing with the feelings that I try to run from. Dealing with my losses in hopes of recovering a small slice of peace.

Learning to dance through shattered glass

Matt,

Thanksgiving is in three days. I'm feeling grief grip my throat. That familiar tightening in my chest has returned. This Thanksgiving feels impossible to survive. My loss and disbelief of living through unfulfilled hopes and dreams feel heavier as the holidays approach.

I've heard the saying about learning to dance in the rain. I feel like I'm navigating life dancing through pieces of shattered glass. Life as I planned for us shattered at my feet the day you died. My life was broken with no chance of ever being repaired.

This season my grief feels heavier. I not only grieve the loss of you, I'm also grieving the loss of me. Of how I hoped Thanksgiving would always be. It's so hard to feel thankful this year. Your empty seat continues to break my heart. My cancer battle has left me with little reserve and feelings of just giving up. It feels like I'm layered in grief. Of wondering how to survive the triggers the holiday season brings.

I have days where I'm so thankful for your life. Days when I feel like I will survive your loss. Days when even my cancer is put on the back burner and I feel joy in the blessings of everyday life. Then I see those painful commercials. The one's of beautiful, happy families celebrating Thanksgiving together. Everyone around the table is smiling. There are no tears of loss. No empty chair where a loved family member will no longer be seated. It's those moments when our reality hits like a cold slap and I want to scream, letting the world know that life isn't as it appears in these fantasy advertisements for how the holidays should be.

It seems the holiday season highlights my grief. Memories of how life used to be unbury themselves from my safe place and resurface, bringing a heightened awareness of my loss. I'm ashamed that my feelings leave me unthankful for the blessings I do have in my life.

The blessings of memories. Remembering our last Thanksgiving together. You and Mike out back bundled up against the cold. Your breath floating above your heads as you shared a memory that brought a smile to both your faces. The blessing of that moment captured in time as I snuck a photo of my two boys together. I look at that photo and feel a mixture of pain and love. How I wish I could blink my eyes and return to that holiday.

The blessing of a loving husband. Ray has been amazing. My broken body is no longer capable of physical activity. Everything I used to do has now fallen on his shoulders. I watch as he walks the dogs down the street. My heart fills with gratitude for this man. He has taken over everything with a smile and a positive attitude of for better or worse.

He sits by my side on those chemo days. He continues to tell me we'll get through this. He is such a gift from God. He held me on days when I sobbed over your loss or cried over losing who I used to be. He reminds me I am still beautiful, with or without my crazy curly hair.

In my brokenness, true friends have shined through my darkness. Rallying around me as I struggle to find a new normal. These women stood by me as I grieved your death and continue to stand by as I battle this cancer. Letting me know they have my back. Being sounding boards when my reality becomes too hard to carry and I need to rant and repeat the things they've all heard before. True friends. Another gift from God.

The blessing of your brother. He understands my grief. He is the only one who really gets what your death has done to our family. We cry together on those days when the grief finds us both.

The holidays hold painful memories that only we share, brothers fighting over the last piece of pumpkin pie. Brothers who would share stories of childhood antics as I cringed at the holiday table. I'm thankful for his presence in my life. His mannerisms are yours. He is the part of you that remains with me.

This holiday season when I'm not feeling so thankful, I will remember these blessing God has placed in my life. I will remember that the holidays, although painful, also hold joy. I will remember our life together. I will shed tears as memories hit but will focus on the light that shines through my darkest days. I will continue to pray for acceptance and peace, knowing I am in control of nothing.

This Thanksgiving, I will give thanks for your life and thanks for those who remain in my life. I will give thanks for the days I feel like I'm human again. I will give thanks for another day of life. I will search for the beauty that finds its way through my brokenness.

Walking the path you walked

Matt,

I feel as though I'm reliving your journey. I remember so clearly your phone call.

"Mom, I was lifting an engine and I felt something in my back pop. The pain is horrible. I can barely walk."

Little did I know that almost five years later, I would be living your experience.

The similarities are mindboggling. You lifted an engine, I lifted a stuck window. As soon as I felt the pop and a searing pain shoot down my leg, I thought of you. They say you can never understand what someone goes through until you go through it yourself. I am a living testimony to that truth.

Looking back, I wish I had known how life-altering your pain was. I never thought it was as horrible as you described. Living with your pain, I now feel so ashamed that I lacked compassion for your pain. All I saw was your addiction to the opioids. Your addiction became my focus. Your pain was a secondary concern.

Now I get it. I'm facing the same surgery you survived. I'm facing trying to find a happy medium to this pain that has become part of my life and a reminder of how you suffered. I'm facing the possibility of becoming addicted as you did after back surgery. I think back to how your life was affected, and I'm terrified that I will become you.

Thursday I will be the patient. I will be you. I will be in the operating room, not the waiting room watching your name flip through the different phases of your surgery. I remember scanning that board every few minutes searching for where you were in the process. I remember walking next to your stretcher to those doors and giving you a kiss for luck. Promising I would be there when you woke. Promising to pray for a successful surgery.

So now I'll be the name Ray and Mike will be following through the surgery. I will be the one with the surgical scar on my back exactly like yours. I remember seeing your scar and feeling chills come over my body. I remember thinking how brave you were to have gone through what you did, never thinking that almost five years after your death, your scar would be on my body.

We have always had this unexplainable connection, you and I. So much alike. Now, even though you are no longer here, I'll be retracing your journey. Feeling your anxiety as you waited for surgery. Understanding your pain as it is now my own.

I pray that I'll feel your presence. That somehow, someway, just for a brief moment, I will know you are there. I pray that neither time nor space will break our connection. I pray that you have forgiven me for not understanding your pain.

Matt's black and white selfie. I always wondered
what he was thinking when he snapped this photo.

YEAR 5

Rogue waves

Matt,

You would think that after five years, I would have a handle on my grief. Maybe a small part of my heart started to believe the myth that time would soften the blow of your death. Maybe to survive I had to think the pain would not always have the crushing power it did in those early days. Perhaps to continue my journey on earth without you I had to live briefly the fantasy that society wants me to believe.

My reality is the polar opposite. This grief continues to hit unexpectedly yet just as powerfully as it always has. I call them rogue waves. I thought that the passing of time would at least soften the edges of my grief. Sadly, I'm finding those edges remain sharp. Like jagged pieces of glass ready to rip my heart to shreds once again.

These waves continue to hit at unexpected times. When I think I've got a shred of control over my emotions, I find quite the opposite.

I don't know if it's the stress of my cancer diagnosis or just the fact that I continue to rethink your struggle with addiction. Perhaps I've got too much time on my hands now as I recover from back surgery and have had to put my advocacy work on the back burner. I'm no longer physically capable of running to meetings or being your voice in Legislative Hall. I'm no longer able to keep my mind busy with changing the broken system that took your life. Time gives my mind the opportunity to relive it all over and over again.

My empathy for your pain is heightened. I now get it. Surgery is no picnic and this recovery has tested my patience. I think about how I just didn't understand your pain. It's like any other situation. Until you live it, you can't get it.

So now my insides churn like an unsettled sea. I feel like I'm being turned inside out. I want to lash out at people who think addiction was your choice. Who think addiction is a moral flaw. My anger rises to the surface when I least expect it. Like those rogue waves, it leaves me struggling to regain control.

I rethink your last days until I can think no more. I want to physically hurt the man who dumped you off at a motel to die rather than doing the right thing by taking you to the hospital or a detox center. I want him to hurt physically and emotionally like your death has hurt me. I want him rotting in jail with no hope of ever seeing the blue sky or hearing the birds sing. I want him to die alone as much as I want you to be alive.

My grief is now multifaceted. I grieve us both. I grieve for what used to be. I grieve the son you once were and the woman I once was. I grieve for the future that could have been but now will never be. I grieve the grandchildren my arms will never hold. I grieve watching my boys grow old together. I grieve the years we have lost, the future we will never share.

My grief and my anger walk hand-in-hand, dancing through my mind. I am helpless to contain either when the reality of life hits with the power of those rogue waves knocking me off my feet, leaving me struggling to find the surface, to catch my breath. Grief is a powerful and never-ending emotion. It does not tell time. It does not conform to society's perception that time softens the blow of death.

I've learned that my grief will last a lifetime. As will my anger over your unnecessary, untimely death. I've learned those waves are out there and will hit again and again. I've learned that I am helpless when they hit and all I can do is ride them to the best of my ability.

Surviving my reality, your death and my cancer, is a challenge. I never saw either coming. I've learned life is fragile and full of unexpected events. I've learned that grief is part of who I am, and will remain part of my life until I cease to be.

Matt with his prized possession. We enjoyed
many days on the bay, away from the crowds.

FEBRUARY 18, 2020

Time doesn't lessen grief, it magnifies it

Matt,

There is a saying that time heals all wounds. People tell you to give it time. Time will help. As if time has magical powers to help you forget that your child is gone. As if they have a clue as to how it feels to walk around with half your heart missing.

All time has done for me is to deepen my already intense pain. All time has done is rob me of the blessing of watching my sons grow old together. Time passes and I realize that I haven't heard your voice or seen your handsome face for five years.

Time is not my friend. Time has become a painful march of family birthdays and holiday celebrations that are no more. Time deepens the grief as reality seeps in, reminding me that this emptiness will be a part of my soul forever.

Weeks have turned to months. Months to years. Yet my grief refuses to loosen its grip on my soul.

Grief has taken over every cell of my body. It pulses through my veins with every beat of my heart, breaking it again as I realize that memories are all I have left of you. Happy times when life was as it should be. Family barbecues, laughter, and love. My two sons enjoying each other's company as siblings do.

But time doesn't have a clue. It marches on and with each new day comes the pain of knowing there will be no phone call or visit today, tomorrow, or forever. Time is like that crack. It starts small and barely noticeable until it transforms into an enormous undeniable rupture separating life into the before and after.

As time passes, people forget. They return to their normal lives, afraid that grief is catchy. Friends disappear into the sunset, running as far and as fast as they can. As if I'm contagious.

Time is a great teacher. It teaches you who gives a damn.

Time does nothing to lessen grief. It does everything to magnify it. I now understand those things I took for granted, like having all the time in the world to say the things I wanted to say, to do the things we dreamed about doing, were never under our control. Time fools you into thinking you will always have more.

Time marches on and doesn't care who it mows down. It has no respect for the grieving heart.

The only thing I want to do with time is have it rewind. Go back to the time when you lived. I call it a do-over. A time when my heart was whole. A time when life held joy and hope, not pain and regret.

Before your death I wanted time to slow down. I complained that time was going by too quickly. Days and months were flying by. I wanted time to give me more moments to enjoy life. To allow the seasons to change slowly so the beauty of each one can linger longer.

Now time can't move fast enough. I want the holidays to fly away and be gone. Birthdays too. I want my head to spin and not have time to know my reality and the pain it continues to bring.

I was never afraid of getting older. I take care of myself. I'm physically active, not bad looking for a sixty-something mom. Aging didn't really bother me, although it does feel like I was only thirty a few days ago. I'm not high maintenance, never worried about a new wrinkle popping up, as I've earned every one being the mother of two boys.

Now I want to close my eyes and be eighty. I want to be closer to the time when I will see you again. I want to see your face and hear your voice. I want to be able to hold you and tell you it's okay.

Matt, you were a beautiful man with a terrible disease. Prior to your death, my time was spent keeping an eye on you. Before your death, time was in short supply. Working and trying to keep you safe took every second of the day. Now time is empty, standing still, endless. Time has also taught me a life lesson. I have no control over it and what it may bring. We've all heard the saying, "In God's time, not ours." Now I finally get it. Time does not belong to us.

The gift of time for me is a double-edged sword. Sharp and cutting one minute, peaceful and too quiet the next. I'm learning that time stops for no one.

For as long as I have left, I will cherish those beautiful memories and wish I knew then what I know now. I would have stayed longer and cherished our time sitting together by the sea.

I would have hugged more and argued less.

I would have fought harder to save you.

Living through time without you is hell. I've read that life isn't a matter of milestones, but of moments.

Until we meet again, I will treasure the moments we've made in the time we had together. Precious moments that time cannot erase.

Looking back through tears

Matt,

It's been a while since I've written. I've thought of you every day but this cancer treatment and two surgeries have really beat me down. I don't even have the energy to cry about everything that's happening to me.

Your loss hits so hard every time I remember you complaining about your back pain after your surgery. Never in a million years could I have ever imagined that your pain would one day invade my body. Like you, I've had the trauma of back surgery and my back is now stabilized with screws and rods.

How I wish you could come back to me for just a few hours. I'd beg your forgiveness for not being more compassionate toward your pain. I always thought you used the surgery as an excuse to take the opioids that finally got you addicted and contributed to your death. I never truly understood how you suffered with every movement every day of your life. All I wanted was get you off the pills so you could get your life back in order.

I guess that saying is true, until you walk in someone's shoes keep your opinion to yourself. I now understand why you never slept in your bed. I would come downstairs to find you sleeping on the couch, TV blaring. I blamed you getting high and falling asleep in positions that looked horribly uncomfortable. I remember waking you up and urging you to go to bed only to have you scowl at me.

Now I get it. I can't believe that I have such a hard time sleeping through the night. I start out in my bed but wake after a few hours in excruciating pain. I need to get up and walk until the pain settles and then I find myself seeking sleep in the recliner, just like I found you.

I've also been given OxyContin. I'll admit I had no choice but to take a few when the pain was unbearable. Every time I handle that prescription bottle, I flash back to you. It is the only thing that helps with the pain but I'm terrified of becoming addicted like you did.

I can't imagine how hard it was for you to continue to live in pain every moment of every day. I feel like God is teaching me a very valueble lesson in empathy. I truly had no idea what you went through until now as I go through the same painful journey after back surgery.

I wish we could go back in time. Knowing what I now know, I would have treated you with compassion instead of expecting you to go to work every day, functioning like a person in perfect shape. Telling you I understand now really makes no difference as you've been gone for five years and two months.

My grief is now wrapped with layers of guilt. Guilt over not being more supportive. Guilt over not helping you find alternative methods to control your pain. Guilt over not being a more loving mother, one whose main concern was for your welfare, not whether you were working or unemployed.

I hope you hear my prayers for you. I hope you know how sorry I am and, most of all, I hope you can forgive me. I've been living with your pain for three months, you lived with this pain for seven years as you also struggled with the horrors of addiction.

There are no words to describe my grief over losing you and now losing who I used to be. I can no longer advocate for the treatment of addiction in our state. I can no longer walk the dogs or do the things that once brought me stress relief and a slice of happiness on those grief-filled days.

This is not the life I envisioned for us. I saw you married with children, living at your happy place by the sea. I saw family vacations with grandkids and grandpups running and jumping in the surf as you and I sat together on the sand sharing the beauty of life. I saw you and Mike growing older together, sharing the joys of fatherhood. I never saw you dying at thirty-seven or me fighting cancer at sixty-three.

I guess it's true, we have no control over how life will twist and turn. That's the hardest to accept. I thought I could save you. Now I'm fighting for my life not knowing what the outcome will be.

We used to sit together by the sea and called it our little slice of heaven. We both felt such peace listening to the waves crashing on the sand. We both felt a connection to God as we sat and marveled at the vastness and beauty of the turquoise sea.

I can only hope that one day we will be together again sitting by the sea we both dearly love. Once again laughing and sharing our joy of being reunited forever. No grief, no guilt, no longer in pain but in paradise. ♥

You are forever in my heart.

Surviving the grief club

Dear reader,

Mothers are not supposed to bury their children. It goes against nature. When a mother loses her young, the world slips off its axis and spins out of control. The universe mourns, knowing it's gone against the circle of life. Children should bury their mothers, not the other way around.

Yet every day, another mother joins our club. The club of the brokenhearted, the club every mother prays to avoid. The club where one day you were whole and the next broken beyond repair. Breath and joy have been sucked out of your body and replaced with a pain so powerful, your soul is lost in the grief. Your world shattered beyond repair. Your child is gone. A victim of a horrible disease. A misunderstood, mistreated disease. The disease that marked them as unworthy and disposable. The disease of addiction.

Your grief is never-ending. It begins each day as you wake and follows you like a lost puppy throughout your day. It crawls into bed with you at night and wraps its arms around your heart. Brief sleep is your only respite. Dreams of your child may come and comfort your heart but when you wake, the nightmare of your life begins anew.

They are your last thought before closing your eyes and the first thought as you awaken. Your child is gone and you remain unable to be comforted.

Your days are now counted out in weeks and months. Last words, hugs, and I love yous are forever burned into your brain. Little things, reminders of your child, can take your breath away without warning. A trip to the grocery store can throw you into a tailspin and leave you struggling to breathe. A bag of chips, a can of Beefaroni, a smell.

You find even the smallest things difficult as your mind remains in shock. Your brain refuses to believe that your child is really gone, knowing that reality will take you to a place of no return. It tricks you into believing they are just away. Things will return to normal when they return home from the beach or treatment.

Your body hurts. Physical pain becomes part of daily living. There are days you feel like you are slowly losing your mind. Your days are spent questioning every decision. You wonder what if. What if I forced him/her into rehab? What if I paid more attention? What if I brought him/her home?

You battle guilt every day. It seeps quietly into your soul. You re-live childhood moments and wonder if you were too harsh, if you loved enough. You sift through memories with a fine-tooth comb, looking for answers to questions that will never be found.

Arguments replay over and over in your mind. You remember and pick apart every word. Things said and those unsaid whirl through your mind. Your brain has become the enemy, refusing to quiet, wishing with every fiber of your being for a do-over. Hindsight slaps your face daily. Knowing what you know now, knowing what you would have done differently. Mothers protect their children. You were unable to protect your child against the demons more powerful than a mother's love.

If you believe, you pray. Every morning and every night. Praying that you are forgiven. Praying for acceptance, peace, guidance, and strength. You ask for signs that your child is finally at peace, their bodies are whole and healthy. Their brains no longer tortured by the demon cravings they were unable to escape while alive. You look to the sky into the clouds yearning to see something that will give you a sense of peace. Cardinals in your yard have new meaning. A song, a sunset, clouds that resemble an angel flood your heart with waves of hope that your child is safe and in a better place.

Your bookshelves now hold books you never thought you would need or receive. Books on losing a child. Books on stages of grief and how to survive each one. Books no mother should ever need to read.

Books written by authors who have survived near-death experiences and tell of bright light and vivid colors. Of peace, happiness and beautiful music. Stories of feeling great love and feelings of being with family. No pain, no fear, no wanting to return to their battered bodies.

Just a peace they never experienced on earth. Books on the afterlife become your bible as you search for answers to the unknown.

Your truth is that you want them back. Living the chaotic roller-coaster life of loving an addict is far better than your reality. The lies, stealing, and everyday chaos seem like a walk in the park when compared to the endless grief that surrounds your world.

You dream of a future that will never be. Meeting girlfriends who become wives. Weddings and birthdays and babies you will never hold in your arms. You close your eyes and go to a world where your heart doesn't hurt. Even for a little while you allow yourself the luxury of a dream. Your world of what-ifs giving you a temporary reprieve from heartache.

Holidays and birthdays now come with gut-punches. You have learned how to avoid the parties. Other mother's plans remind you of your loss, your family now broken. Old traditions are too painful to continue. New traditions feel like a betrayal to your child. Family pictures are now missing the face you long to see. Your mind tells you to move on, your heart says no.

Friends have gone back to their lives, back to their living children. Calls and visits become less frequent as they leave you alone with your grief. You learn that being alone is better than feeling like a stranger in a room full of people who are afraid to look your way. Afraid to speak your child's name. Afraid that someday they will be you. Their excuse of not knowing what to say gets old as you learn to accept your solitude. True friends shine like diamonds on your dark days. You can count them on one hand.

You are trying to find new meaning for your life. Your loss has left a void as deep as the ocean. Your time was spent trying to save your child. You are angry, and battle acceptance.

The stages of grief warn you that these feelings will come. Your anger is directed not toward your child but toward the stigma that continues to follow your grief. The stigma that shows on the faces of people when they hear the word overdose. Not sympathy, but looks of accusation, as if you caused the disease. You refuse to accept their ignorance. They run away not wanting it to touch their lives. You are the black sheep in the flock. Your reality is their nightmare.

Your anger becomes your strength, your loss becomes your passion. You find a voice you never knew existed. Your soul comes alive, fueling itself off your grief. Your pain pushes you toward a path that becomes your new purpose.

Your journey is to honor your child. To fight against the system that broke, then killed you both. To prevent another mother's heartbreak. Your hands on education makes you expert in this disease.

You are the mother of all mothers. You loved and lost your child. You are their voice. You are their warrior. Their fight is over. Yours has begun. You are the mother of an addict. You will not be silenced.

In loving memory of my son, Matt.

ACKNOWLEDGMENTS

This book would have never been possible without the love and support from my family and friends. First, I must thank my incredible husband, Ray. He was my rock through Matt's full-blown addiction, never once stopping me from doing what I needed to do to try to save Matt. Always encouraging me to do what I needed to do. Never once telling me to choose between our marriage and my son.

Since Matt's death, Ray continues to allow me the gift to grieve, never once making me feel guilty as the years passed and my tears continued to fall. He has supported me through these last five years with love and compassion. I would never have survived this journey without his support.

My son, Mike, has been my voice of reason. When the guilt hits and the what-ifs and should-haves hammer my heart, he reassures me I did everything humanly possible to help his younger brother find recovery. We share a grief that surpasses time and space.

My dearest friends JoAnn, Pat, and Debbie, who have supported me throughout my grief journey. They never tire of Matt stories. They have held me when the grief waves hit, and allow me to remove my mask and just be a grieving mother. They are the remaining three who have not abandoned me because I continue to grieve my son.

My precious pups, who licked the tears off my face and gathered around me on those dark days. Their unconditional love during those first weeks helped me survive many sleepless nights.

I also thank the parents who joined my support group, Support After Addiction Death. We share a bond no parent would ever sign up for. We get it. We need no words. We're each other's lifeline when those anniversaries bring us to our knees. Once strangers, we have become family.

I also want to thank Lynda Cheldelin Fell for taking her time to encourage me to take that step toward fulfilling my dream of publishing my letters to Matt.

Finally, I thank God for giving me the beautiful gift of words. I've read that when God closes one door, He opens another. Before Matt's death, I could not write anything worth reading. After his death the words flowed from my soul. I would sit at my computer and pray to God for the words to touch people's hearts. This book is a product of God's blessings.

Even when I could not feel his presence, He was with me.

MARYBETH CICHOCKI

ABOUT MARYBETH CICHOCKI

MaryBeth Cichocki is a retired registered nurse living in Delaware. She lost her youngest son, Matt, to an overdose of prescription drugs on January 3, 2015.

After his death, she was unable to return to her world of taking care of critically ill babies in the NICU. She now spends her time advocating and writing about the disease of addiction. She started a blog shortly after Matt died titled Mothers Heart Break, which tells the story of Matt's addiction and continues into the present as she deals with complicated grief.

MaryBeth also facilitates SADD, a support group for those who have suffered the loss of a loved one to the disease of addiction.

MaryBeth has testified in her state capitol at the Joint Finance Committee hearings, sharing her story of the difficulty she experienced while trying to find comprehensive treatment for her adult son during his addiction. She works with legislators in her state to implement changes in how the disease of substance use disorder will be treated in the future. She played a pivotal role in the passing of six bills in Delaware related to treatment for those suffering from substance abuse disease.

MaryBeth is passionate about saving other mothers from her grief. She is a wife, mother, grandmother, and dog rescuer.

CONTACT:

EMAIL: mecichocki@gmail.com

BLOG: mothersheartbreak.com

ALYBLUE MEDIA TITLES

PARTIAL LIST

Survivors

Faces of Resilience

Barely Breathing

Who Took Molly Bish?

She, He & Finding Me

Color My Soul Whole

Remembering My Child

My Grief Diary

Grammy Visits From Heaven

Grandpa Visits From Heaven

Daddy Visits From Heaven

Faith, Grief & Pass the Chocolate Pudding

Crimson Sunshine

Heaven Talks to Children

A Child is Missing: A True Story

A Child is Missing: Searching for Justice

Grief Reiki

Hidden Truths Within

Where have all the children gone?

GRIEF DIARIES

Surviving Loss by Overdose

Surviving Sudden Loss

Through the Eyes of a Widow

Surviving Loss by Cancer

Surviving Loss of a Spouse

Surviving Loss of a Child

Surviving Loss of a Sibling

Surviving Loss of a Parent

Surviving Loss of an Infant

Surviving Loss of a Loved One

Surviving Loss by Suicide

Surviving Loss of Health

How to Help the Newly Bereaved

Surviving Loss by Impaired Driving

Surviving Loss by Homicide

Surviving Loss of a Pregnancy

Hello from Heaven

Grieving for the Living

Shattered

Project Cold Case

Poetry & Prose and More

Through the Eyes of Men

Will We Survive?

Victim Impact Statement

Hit by Impaired Driver

Surviving Loss of a Pet

REAL LIFE DIARIES

Living with a Brain Injury

Through the Eyes of DID

Through the Eyes of an Eating Disorder

Living with Endometriosis

Living with Mental Illness

Living with Rheumatic Disease

Living with Gastroparesis

Through the Eyes of a Funeral Director

INTERNATIONAL GRIEF INSTITUTE

Aftercare Solutions Manual

iCare Grief Support Group Facilitator Manual

iCare Grief Support Participant Workbook

iCare Church Support Facilitator Manual

iCare Church Support Participant Workbook

iCare Grief Ministry Guide

iCare Grief Ministry Workbook

iCare Chapter Leader Manual

iCare Chapter Workbook

Resilience Rx: Compassion Fatigue

iCare Booklet Series

PUBLISHED BY ALYBLUE MEDIA
Real stories. Real people. Real hope.
www.AlyBlueMedia.com

Made in the USA
Middletown, DE
27 November 2021

53003347R00183